THE BARANYA DISPUTE
1918–1921
Diplomacy in the Vortex of Ideologies

LESLIE CHARLES TIHANY

EAST EUROPEAN QUARTERLY, BOULDER
DISTRIBUTED BY COLUMBIA UNIVERSITY PRESS
NEW YORK

1978

EAST EUROPEAN MONOGRAPHS, NO. XXXV

by the same author

A History of Middle Europe, Rutgers University Press,
New Brunswick, N.J., 1976

Copyright © 1978 by East European Quarterly
Library of Congress Card Catalogue Number 77-82389
ISBN 0-914710-28-1

Printed in the United States of America

Foreword

This book is about the breakup of empires and the social chaos when ideologies clash. The scene is Eastern Europe early in our century. During the Nineteenth Century, secession, as an idea and an act, had been as American as apple pie. New England toyed with the idea at the Hartford Convention in 1814; the Confederacy unsuccessfully tried the act in 1861–65. In 1903 the United States jubilantly welcomed the Panamanian breakaway from Colombia making possible an American canal where the French had failed. In all three instances the secessionist idea sprouted in the minds of regionalists who dissented from the policies pursued by the national center. They sought — unsuccessfully like the Confederates or successfully in the case of the isthmians — protection and recognition from abroad to buttress independence.

At the end of World War I the secessionist scene shifted to Central and Eastern Europe. The empires of the Czars and of the Hapsburg emperors burst at the seams under the centrifugal pull of separatist forces. New states emerged and declared their ephemeral independence in the middle of a continent near anarchy because of Bolshevik power in Russia. In the Twentieth Century Balkans, the secessionist pattern was essentially the same as it had been in the New World during the preceding century. Breakaway was preceded by irreconcilable disagreement on the principle of national self-determination — a new ethnic variation of states' rights elaborated by the Virginian Woodrow Wilson. The struggle between Western and Eastern ideologies complicated the political process. Did it behoove an anti-Bolshevik state (it did!) to further its territorial ambitions by spreading a protective umbrella over the Moscow-affiliated secessionists of a neighbor who was anti-Communist? These newest secessionists still sought external protection by offering a natural resource: coal instead of cotton or an interoceanic route. Decidedly new, however, was the behavioral pendulum accelerated by historical change. In Baranya, the territory disputed between Hungary and Yugoslavia in 1918–21, the secessionists of one day became the unionists of the next, and vice versa. Power in the national center shifted from the hands of ideological friend to the grasp of political foe.

During the age of geographical discoveries it was common for explorers to come upon uncharted islands. In modern historiography this is a rare occurrence for the researchers who record and analyze political-economic phenomena. In Twentieth Century diplomatic history the surfacing, in this book, of the Baranya dispute is similar to the discovery of an unmarked and small but geologically significant island in the course of an ocean voyage. Future textbooks in the field will no longer be able to leave unmentioned that in the wake of World War I a seceding city republic in Central Europe, emerging from the ideological vortex of nationalism and socialism, was consigned to historical oblivion by the concerted diplomatic action of the concerned Great Powers.

The events of 1918–21 in Baranya have been brought to light and their meaning for the present explained by Professor Tihany. But for the future also an understanding of what happened after World War I at this crossroads of invasions may be important. The very same north-Yugoslav border which is the scene of events unfolding in this book, may once again serve in the near future as an ideological battleground between local nationalisms and Soviet Communism as the historical exit of a venerable regional ruler inexorably approaches.

Professor Leslie Tihany was qualified on three counts to write this interesting, scholarly book. He is an experienced diplomat who spent nearly thirty years in the service of the State Department and the U.S. Foreign Service; he is a historian of note trained in leading American universities; he is an eyewitness to some of the events and thoroughly familiar with the area he describes. It is a source of pride that Dr. Tihany performed his research in facilities provided by the City of Cincinnati and its renowned university.

Luke Feck
Editor
The Cincinnati Enquirer

November 9, 1977

Contents

APPENDIXES:

"Turning and turning in the widening gyre
The falcon cannot hear the falconer;
Things fall apart; the centre cannot hold;
Mere anarchy is loosed upon the world. . ."

W. B. Yeats, *The Second Coming* (1921)

Acknowledgments

This book was made possible thanks to the opening of long-sealed archives by the French Ministry of Foreign Affairs in 1972. The files of telegrams, despatches, and other communications made available in Paris complemented, controlled, and balanced the version of the Baranya dispute based on documentation preserved in the archives of the Municipality of Pécs in Hungary. My former employer, the United States Foreign Service, allowed me to spend enough time on leave both in Pécs (in 1967) and in Paris (during 1969–1971) to acquire and locate in advance materials already published in Pécs, and the dossiers not yet accessible in Paris, on which my monograph is based. The laborious task of winnowing and sifting through the newly released French and Allied diplomatic correspondence fell to the unflagging lot of my French brother, Hugues-Jean de Dianoux, *Conseiller d'Ambassade,* who happened to arrive on home leave in Paris from his Foreign Service shortly after my return to the United States for retirement.

Microfilms of the materials gathered by M. de Dianoux were purchased for the Hoover Institution on War, Revolution, and Peace, and placed at my disposal, by the Institution's Chief Archivist and Senior Fellow, Dr. Milorad M. Drachkovitch, to whom I am additionally indebted for sharing with me family memories of his father's assassination during the Baranya dispute. As Yugoslav Minister of the Interior, the elder Dr. Drachkovitch is one of the *dramatis personae* who appear in my monograph.

Former Hungarian Prime Minister Dr. Ferenc Nagy and former Hungarian Lieutenant General Kálmán Hardy, both eyewitnesses of the 1918–1921 Baranya events, graciously communicated to me their reminiscences in writing.

The Department of Slavic Languages and Literatures of the Library of Congress gave me high-caliber research assistance by locating and reproducing primary source materials unavailable to me in my bucolic Ohio Valley retreat. I was able to visit and to work to good advantage in the Library of the University of Cincinnati, where I received courteous and efficient staff help.

Several of my colleagues, especially Professors Thomas Sakmyster, Alfonz Lengyel, and Adalberto Pinelo, came to my rescue when *vis maior* temporarily isolated me from bibliographic and technical facilities. Professor William M. McKim suggested the Yeats quotation as a fitting epigraph for my book. Mr. James S. Bowman, Clerk of the Session of the First Presbyterian Church of Fort Thomas, Kentucky, generously provided me with office and study space in which to work undisturbed. My wife Maria, a former foreign affairs research analyst in the United States Department of State, helped me greatly with statistical research and with Serbo-Croatian linguistic problems.

To all the foregoing my sincere thanks.

Preface

If, as a result of a lost war, the State of Arizona fell under military occupation from south of the border, while in unoccupied Washington revolutionary and counterrevolutionary governments of the Left and Right followed each other in rapid succession, patriotic loyalties at both ends of the political spectrum would probably be put to a severe test in Arizona. Would nationalism have priority over Marxism-Leninism or *vice versa?* What would be the preconditions of political fusion and fission between the two? The desire of local conservatives to be reunited with the mother country might well be tempered by a wait-and-see attitude during the time a leftist government rules in the national capital. Conversely, with the Left in control on the Potomac, nothing would prevent the radicals in occupied territory from pursuing a "union must be saved" policy under banners calling on the proletarians of the country to reunite. However, the replacement of a leftist by a rightist regime in the distant national center could easily reverse the local political stances: the Left shifting from unionism to separatism in order to prevent the extension of rightist rule to its own microcosm; the antithetic Right abandoning separatism to re-embrace unionism under a national government of its own ideological persuasion.

During these political gyrations the occupying power could be expected to pursue its own strategic objectives. First, it would probably shift and throw its backing to whatever local faction is momentarily anti-unionist and secessionist. Second, it would reasonably attempt to gain converts among the indigenous population of the occupied territory for annexation by the state south of the border. The unstable political situation might be further complicated by the heedlessness of the occupiers to the global policy lines laid down by the great powers of the victorious coalition which had made the local occupation possible. The flux of ideologies — nationalism and socialism — would therefore in the final analysis be subject in the occupied area to three external factors: the governmental see-saw in the distant national center; the regional objectives pursued by the occupiers, and the overriding veto of the victorious great powers.

A farfetched hypothetical situation? An Orwellian nightmare? Historical antecedents are not lacking. Think of sixteenth-century England fluctuating between Catholicism and Protestantism, with Spanish occupying forces in Ireland toward the end of Elizabeth's reign; or more recently, of the predicament experienced by French residents and administrators in Syria-Lebanon or Indochina while Vichy and the Free French were contending for mastery over France. But the final formula of the preceding paragraph, the flux of political ideologies in an imaginary national emergency is clearly and demonstrably applicable to an actual, and possibly paradigmatic precedent, which arose at the end of World War I on the southern peripheries of the defeated Austro-Hungarian Empire. The purpose of this monograph is to narrate and analyze for the first time, on the basis of unresearched archival materials and memoirs, the events that took place between 1918 and 1921 in the Yugoslav-occupied parts of the Hungarian county of Baranya, while — in the words of Yeats — things fell apart, the center could not hold, the falcon could not hear the falconer, and mere anarchy was loosed upon the world.

The paradigmatic value — if any — of the Baranya precedent is probably heightened by a coincident circumstance. The end of World War I ushered in an age of which the end is still not in sight, of vertical world conflicts obscuring the earlier, relatively simple strategic phenomenon of sovereign states engaged in horizontal warfare across international frontiers for dynastic or national interests. Beginning with World War I horizontal wars (Germans against Russians) have shown a tendency to continue as vertical conflicts (Reds against Whites) within national boundaries among population elements grouped according to particular domestic interests, as revolutionary struggles and civil wars for self-assertion between historically dominant and traditionally subordinate classes respectively embattled for and against the internal status quo.

The time was prophetically out of joint during 1918–1921 in the Baranya microcosm, the traditional gateway between Central Europe and the Balkans. It was the author's dubious privilege as an observant schoolboy to be introduced to history and politics in this time of troubles. What he saw then from the edge of crowds and from windows featherbedded to stop stray bullets, is now presented to the reader in the following pages with the help of skills, tools, and documentation he has acquired since.

Cincinnati, Ohio   L.C.T.
1977

Introduction

In the spring of 1921 — on March 7, March 17, and again on May 5 — two unfamiliar place names, Baranya[1] and Pécs[2] echoed in the House of Lords. The occasions were debates concerning the delayed ratification process of the fourth peace treaty ending the First World War, the Treaty of Trianon with Hungary, which had been signed in the Trianon Palace of Versailles on June 4, 1920 but had not yet entered into force. "The district of Baranya and the town of Pécs," Lord Newton said, are

> . . . portions of Hungary [which] are at this moment occupied by Serbian forces who, in flagrant contradiction to agreement and flagrant opposition to the dictates of the Allies, have set up a civil form of Government which is Bolshevist in its character and extremely detrimental to this unfortunate country. What makes the case worse is that the occupied district is the only portion of Hungary in which there is any coal left.[3]

Lord Newton's was a simple formulation of the Baranya problem, consonant with the historical frame of reference and the spirit of the times. Half a century later, in a different historical frame of reference and in a changed spirit of the times, in the People's Republic of Hungary, the post-World War I Baranya developments were summarized in the following manner:

> *Baranya Republic.* An attempt in August 1921 by the workers of [the city of] Pécs and Baranya to prevent the entry of Horthyist[4] troops. During November 1918 a large part of Baranya County was occupied by Yugoslav[5] troops. Progressive forces held in check the implementation of open efforts at annexation and made secure in this area the achievements of the [Hungarian] bourgeois democratic revolution [of October 1918]. After the overthrow of the [Hungarian] Soviet Republic [in August 1919] this territory became a safehaven for refugees fleeing the White Terror. After the Treaty of Trianon [of June 4, 1920] awarded the larger part of Baranya County to Hungary, the leaders of the workers in the occupied territories and of the city of Pécs (in August 1920 the municipality of Pécs had a Socialist majority) decided on the proclamation of the Baranya Republic in order to

prevent the entry of Horthyist troops. This [proclamation] took place on August 14, 1921. The painter Peter Dobrovits was elected President of the Executive Committee of the Republic. The Yugoslav Government, motivated by annexionist ideas, was inclined to support the Baranya Republic but was compelled, under the pressure of the Great Powers, to evacuate this territory on August 20, 1921. The Baranya Republic ceased to exist after a duration of one week.[6]

More than half a century has now passed since Magyars and Serbs came to terms and Baranya ceased to be an international problem. Yet era and area are both still *terra incognita* to historians. It may be therefore a modest contribution, in the perspective of fifty years, to write not only a history of the clash between Magyars and Serbs over Baranya but also to analyze the flux of the two principal ideologies of our day — nationalism and socialism — in this totally unexplored Middle-European microcosm.

I

The Baranya Territory

1. *Area and Population*

As Austria-Hungary entered World War I in July 1914, Baranya was one of sixty-three Hungarian counties *(megye)*. It was situated in the Danube-Drava triangle of western Hungary, bordering on the Associated Kingdom of Croatia in the south, the Hungarian county of Somogy in the west, and the Hungarian county of Bács-Bodrog (Bachka) across the south-flowing Danube in the east. The area of Baranya County in 1914 covered 5,106 square kilometers (1,963 square miles). In size therefore the prewar county was somewhat smaller than the State of Delaware. According to the Hungarian census of 1911, Baranya at the end of 1909 had a total population of 299,312, which was decreasing owing to overseas emigration, mostly to the United States.[1]

The breakdown[2] of the same census shows a heterogeneous population, which spoke the following languages as a mother tongue:

Hungarian	149,083	(51.3%)
German	103,334	(35.5%)
Croatian	14,622	(5%)
Serbian	12,743	(4%)
Slovak	267	
Ruthenian	7	
Other	10,686	

Of the population speaking as a mother tongue languages other than Hungarian, 47,801 spoke the latter tongue as a second language.[3] Thus 85% of the population was Hungarian-speaking in 1909. Speakers of Serbo-Croatian were, however, in a majority in the apex of the Danube-Drava triangle, south of a line drawn from the village of Kiskőszeg on the Danube to a point near the hamlet of Bolmány on the Drava river. Seventy percent of the county population over six years of age, and 60.9% of the total county population, was literate.[4]

Religion[5] was another indicator of the heterogeneous character of the population, which was divided among the following denominations:

Roman Catholic	216,490	(74.5%)
Reformed (Calvinist)	41,559	(14.3%)
Evangelical (Lutheran)	13,203	(4.5%)
Eastern Orthodox	13,337	(4.6%)
Jewish	5,287	(1.8%)
Other (not including Greek Catholic and Unitarian)	685	

Of the county's labor force 48% were engaged in agriculture; 37%, in mining and industry; 12% were artisans and craftsmen; 1.5% were employed in communication and transportation; 1.5%, in commerce.[6] The relatively high percentage of industry-mining sector employees was an indicator of the rich anthracite coal mines situated in the center of the county (1911 production: seven million hundredweights per annum)[7] and to the presence of several well-developed industries in and around Pécs, the county seat. There were 34 large-size industrial enterprises, including the Zsolnay ceramics plant, the Littke champagne distillery, the Hirschfeld (Pannonia) brewery, the Höffler tannery, the Hamerli leather goods shops, the Angster organ-building factory, and others.[8]

The city of Pécs, picturesquely situated on the southern slope of the Mecsek massif (highest peak: 1,146 feet), had in 1909 a population of 49,882,[9] which had decreased to 47,556 by 1920. Statistics for 1911 showed the following demographic divisions in the city:

According to Mother Tongue:[10]

Hungarian	41,620
German	6,356
Croatian	688
Czech	521
Slovak	162
Serbian	125
Other	342

According to Religion:[11]

Roman Catholic	42,653
Reformed (Calvinist)	1,173
Evangelical (Lutheran)	1,123
Jewish	4,026

According to Occupation[12] (in 1920):

Total City Population	47,556
Labor Force	22,642
Total Number of Manual Workers	10,476
Total Number of Miners	1,396
Miners Resident beyond City Limits	3,025

Pécs was the seat of a Roman Catholic Bishop. Plans to restore its university, founded in 1367, were interrupted by the war. In peacetime two regiments were stationed in and near the town: the Nineteenth *Honvéd* (Hungarian Territorial Defense) Infantry Regiment, and the first squadron of the Eighth *Honvéd* Hussar Regiment. As the war progressed, a company of yet another regiment was billeted on the outskirts of the city, the Sixth *"K und K"* (Imperial and Royal, in other words, mixed Austro-Hungarian) Infantry Regiment. The effectives of the Nineteenth and Eighth Regiments were predominantly Hungarian; those of the Sixth, Serbian.

2. *Brief History to World War I*

At the dawn of history Baranya and the urban predecessors of Pécs were occupied by warlike Illyrian tribes, known as *Pannonii* to the Romans, who incorporated them and their territory into the Pannonian province of their empire in A.D. 8.[13] The city of Pécs was built on Celtic foundations. During the period of migrations at the time of the fall of the Roman Empire, the Romanized Illyrian-Celtic population of the province was swept away or submerged in irrupting hordes of Huns (fourth and fifth centuries), Slavs (fifth and sixth centuries), Avars (mid-sixth century), and Magyars or Hungarians (ninth century).[14] The latter drove a wedge between the Western Slavs (Czechs, Slovaks, and Poles) and South Slavs (Croatians, Serbs, and Bulgarians). The Hungarians established a kingdom (1001), of which Baranya and Pécs were still part as the first world war was drawing to a close in 1918. From 1526 to 1689 the county and the town were under Ottoman Turkish occupation. The fateful battle of Mohács (1526), which marked the end of an independent Hungarian kingdom and its absorption in the empire of the Habsburgs, was fought on Baranya soil. The South Slav population element (Croatians and Serbians) came fleeing before the approaching Turkish invaders from the fifteenth to the eighteenth centuries, but some of the place names date back to the vanished pre-Hungarian Slavic population of the fifth to the ninth centuries. The German ethnic element was formed of descendants of colonists invited by the Habsburg king-emperors after the final expulsion of the Turks around 1700.[15] The German settlers of that period came from the Upper Rhine, Franconia, Schleswig-Holstein, Württemberg, Baden, the Black Forest, and Hesse-Nassau.[16] The four-towered cathedral which dominates Pécs (known as Sopianae to the Romans, Quinque Ecclesiae to medieval populations, Fünfkirchen to the Germans, and Pechuy to the South Slavs) was begun over fourth-century Christian catacombs under the first kings of Hungary in the eleventh century. It burnt down in 1064; was rebuilt in the twelfth century; and then underwent a complete restructuring in 1882–1891 to a style in which the outbreak of World War I found it.[17]

3. Sociography of the City of Pécs

Pécs and its surrounding mining area had a radical reputation in conservative, pre-World War I Hungary. The town was already known around 1900 as a "nest of reds."[18] The mines were owned by the Danube Steamship Navigation Company (DGHT), in which the ruling Habsburg family was the majority stockholder, while a minority of shares were owned by British interests.[19] Employer-employee relationship in an age of nearly unbridled capitalism was thus further envenomed by deeply-rooted political antagonism to the ultraconservative establishment ruling from Vienna and Budapest. A considerable percentage of the miners were first- or second-generation immigrants — Germans, Austrians, Wends, and Croatians — most of whom knew collective bargaining from their homelands and, lacking deep roots in Hungary, could without too much trouble face a renewed migratory existence should a clash with the authorities require it.[20]

Pécs was the only industrial town in Hungary with mines in its immediate peripheries. The farthest shafts (Vasas) were only 20 kilometers distant from the center of town. This proximity made for symbiosis and close cooperation between the suburban miners and the urban industrial proletariat. It was perhaps due to this combination of forces that the first miners' union in Hungary was organized, and permitted by the authorities, in Pécs.[21] The emergence of this early union began during a miners' strike in 1893, which was suppressed by the police but out of which grew a camouflaged miners' union under the name "Workers' Educational Association" (Munkásképző Egylet).[22] By 1900 the authorities were ready to issue a permit for a regular trade union, and the educational masque could be cast away. Renewed labor trouble and sporadic strikes in the Pécs mines (one lasting 55 days in 1905), however, led to the suppression of the union in December 1906. In closing the union, the authorities confiscated its entire treasury of 1,898.60 crowns.[23] But the miners continued to lead an organized existence underground until the end of 1918, when the newly-risen bourgeois-revolutionary government under Michael Károlyi granted legality to their union.

Another radical "first" in Pécs took place in 1911, when the Baranya county seat became the first Hungarian city to elect members of the Social Democratic Party (SDP), founded in 1890, to its municipal council.[24] The policies of the SDP — which remained without representation in the Hungarian parliament until after World War I — were determined by the rapidly multiplying trade unions. By the end of 1905, not counting the miners, there were 2,299 organized workers in Pécs (out of a national total of 71,163). By 1911 union membership in and around the town increased to 2,528 (out of a national total of 95,180); by 1913, to 6,299 (out of a national total of 107,486).[25] In 1914, just before the outbreak of the war, there was a miners' strike of eight weeks in Pécs.[26] The war continued, seemingly indefinitely. Proletarian discontent was in ferment. In January 1918 an industrial workers' strike of large proportions took place in the town. Roving bands of strikers were singing the latest wartime folksong:

> Cold winds are blowing from Russia,
> They bring the message:
> The great Russian Czar has lost his power!
> The great Russian Czar has lost his power!

But Pécs was not only "red," it was also "black" in the Stendhalian sense. At the other end of the political spectrum from the proletarian malcontents were the powerful and influential clericals grouped around the diocesan Roman Catholic bishop. During and after the war years the Bishop of Pécs was Count Julius Zichy, scion of an aristocratic family. In the heart of the city stood a baroque monument to the Holy Trinity, elevating the sculptured image of the Host for all inhabitants, fidel and infidel. Within a stone's throw of the monument stretched the imposing facade of the Cistercian Gymnasium (classical High School), one of the best in Hungary. There were also a seminary, a monastery, a convent, a law academy, a multitude of churches, and a large army of priests, monks, and nuns, all wearing their distinctive and characteristic garb. The diocese was very rich. The landed estates of the episcopal see and of the cathedral chapter covered about 100,000 cadastral *holds* (one Hungarian *hold* equals 1.42 acres).[27] The estates and the various institutions provided a livelihood for a whole corps of ecclesiastical intendants, stewards, professors, teachers, clerks, foresters, architects, viticulturists, cellarers, artisans, manual workers, purchasers, agents, sales personnel, etc.

At the turn of the century, as a counterweight to the new Social Democratic Party, the diocese began sponsoring Christian Socialist trade unions.[28] During the immediate prewar years Pécs turned into a waiting battleground of Socialist and clerical forces. It became a city divided against itself, polarized and stamped with a *rouge et noir* character, except — unlike in Stendhal's classic — *rouge* here symbolized not the army but the proletarian host of the town. This clerical-socialist antithesis seemed more pronounced in Pécs than anywhere else in Hungary. The polarization probably accounted for the fact that the proletariat of the Pécs area gradually assumed a militantly and intransigently anti-establishment stance. Conversely, the conservative, clergy-centered bourgeoisie grew into an uncompromising upholder of the status quo, rigidly resisting the demands of leftist labor. On the eve of the war a "throne and altar" type of patriotism characterized the clerical Right. When war was declared, the SDP and the trade unions could not resist the sweep of fervent nationalism and pledged their support of the military effort. But as the war dragged on and the soviets began their rise to power in Russia, the Socialist Left in Pécs seemed to be taking the road of proletarian internationalism. Two hostile camps and two antagonistic ideologies were waiting in Baranya for the coming trial of strength.

II

The Dissolution of Austria-Hungary in Baranya

1. *Mutiny of the Sixth Regiment*

One of the earliest symptoms of the impending collapse of the Central Powers occurred in Pécs on May 20, 1918. This was the Whitsuntide Mutiny of the Sixth Imperial and Royal Infantry Regiment[1] — the first armed uprising during World War I on the territory of the old Hungarian Kingdom. The Sixth was a predominantly Serbian military unit, normally headquartered in the then Hungarian Bachka (now Yugoslav Voyvodina) region between the Danube and the Tisza rivers. It was a veteran, battle-scarred fighting force; many of its effectives had spent months or years in Russian prisoner-of-war camps; were freed and returned to their Austro-Hungarian command after the Russian October Revolution of 1917; and had now received orders to entrain for the Italian front on the morning of May 21. Their scheduled departure for the bloody battles of the Italian campaign was to follow by one day the Whitsuntide picnic, dance, and general merriment of the Hungarian-staffed Fifty-second *Honvéd* Infantry Regiment announced for the Tettye resort area on the pleasant green heights above the city. The mainsprings of the mutiny lay, therefore, not only in the battleweariness and defeatism of soldiers who had witnessed the beginnings of the Russian Revolution, but also in the basic ethnic animosities of the multinational Habsburg Monarchy.

The mutiny of the Sixth began early in the morning of May 20 within the walls of the suburban Archduke Frederick Barracks. The first signs were apparently unorganized demonstrations during which disaffected privates and noncoms swarmed onto the parade grounds shouting demands to end the war. There were loud cries of refusal to leave for the front and a chorus of voices praising the enemy country Serbia. A band of excited soldiers entered the duty officer's cubicle and ordered him to hand over the keys to the arsenal, the munition dumps, and the regimental treasury. The duty officer replied with a pistol shot and was immediately bayoneted to death. All his keys were taken. Arms including twenty machineguns were seized. Within a few minutes 1,500 armed men took over the barracks, arrested (and in several instances shot) their officers, placed themselves under the command of trusted noncoms, and began occupying other buildings. These included the main and suburban railroad stations, and the White Wolf Tavern, where the mutineers set up their headquarters. Machinegun emplacements were erected at surrounding street corners; an armed patrol was sent to the mining area to invite the presumably sympathetic miners to join in the uprising.

While the patrol was on its way to its destination beyond the city limits, a counterattack by loyal troops was launched from the center of the town. The first foray against the machinegun nests of the mutineers was made by the Eighth Hussars, with catastrophic results resembling the charge of the Light Brigade. Soon the asphalt sidewalks were strewn with bodies of mounts and riders. The Nineteenth Infantry was next brought up, wheeling machineguns. Now a stalemate developed, a stationary firefight between the mutineers, who held their positions, and the loyalists, who barred the way to the center of the town, but could not advance toward the White Wolf Tavern or the barracks. Suddenly news arrived that a company of the Ninth *Honvéd* Infantry Regiment was approaching Pécs by train, on its way to the fighting front, equipped with mountain artillery. The troop train was stopped before it could reach the rebel-held depots. The Ninth was brought into action with its artillery pieces. It was all over by mid-afternoon. The White Wolf Tavern, near the present university grounds, looked like a discarded sieve, its walls perforated with gaping holes. The most resolute mutineers, as in the Paris Commune nearly half a century earlier, found their way to a nearby cemetery, where they made their last stand among the graves and tombstones.

News of the mutiny had reached the miners in their homes before the patrol could get to them. Wishful thinking prevailed: not only the Sixth Regiment but the entire Pécs garrison were thought to be in revolt; the war was over; the miners should obtain arms to join the mutinous soldiers. But how and where? The area of the mines was guarded by a military detachment with a command post and a detention pen for recalcitrant miners. The detachment was quickly disarmed. A miner's son, a corporal, home on furlough, broke into the stockade at the head of a handful of newly-armed men, liberated the prisoners, gave them weapons, and attacked the command post. The Lieutenant Colonel and Captain holding it were captured. A march began toward Pécs to hand the two officers over to the rebellious soldiery wrongly assumed to be in control of the town. A short distance outside the city limits the miners and the military patrol sent by the mutineers came face to face. They fraternized. It took the soldiers only a few minutes to convince their new civilian allies that military justice could be rendered on the spot. Without further ado the two officers were lined up against a wall and summarily executed by an improvised firing squad.

It was only after the double execution that a reserve officer, a lawyer and a socialist organizer in civilian life, arrived in the miners' tenements with a realistic situation report. The mutiny in Pécs had been quelled; the miners should — and immediately did — throw away their arms to avoid severe reprisals. These were not late in coming. In the courtyard of the City Hall the hands of captives, military and civilian, were sniffed for the smell of gunpowder. A court martial, divided into eight sections for speedier work, began trying the captured mutineers. The first day four soldiers found guilty were shot before a large and curious public on a military parade ground. Eight more military were executed during the next few days. The trials of the civilians, mostly miners, took several years and resulted in one death sentence. Other defendants received prison terms of various durations. Survivors were freed during the following autumn after the collapse of the old régime and the establishment of the new bourgeois-democratic government.[2]

From local mutiny to general débacle was only a matter of a few months. The military uprising in Pécs marked the beginning of the end for the Central Powers' war effort. As the moment of inevitable defeat approached, the center could not hold and centrifugal forces long at work in the Habsburg Monarchy exploded the Empire to its component parts. Chaos and other revolts followed in the wake of the Sixth Regiment's mutiny in Pécs. No published evidence indicates awareness by Allied intelligence of how the seams began to burst in Baranya during the spring of 1918.

2. *The Postwar Political Metabolism*

The north-to-south troop movements through Baranya during May 1918 were preparatory to the last great Austro-Hungarian military effort of the war: the Piave offensive in Italy (June 15–24, 1918). The gamble failed and cost the reeling Dual Monarchy 100,000 casualties. But this was not the only blow. On September 30 the Bulgarian front cracked in the Balkans and the road lay open for a northward Allied advance from the Aegean to the Danube. Serbian troops spearheading the French-led Allied offensive re-entered their capital Belgrade on

November 1. Within the following two weeks they crossed the frontier at several points into Hungary. On November 3 the Dual Monarchy sought and was granted by the Allies an armistice at Padua. Acting as an independent state for the first time since 1849, Hungary signed a separate Military Convention with the Allies in Belgrade on November 13, 1918.[3] The formal declaration of independence was issued in Budapest on November 16. The Dual Monarchy was no more; by mutual agreement Austria and Hungary loosed the bonds which had united them since 1540. The Belgrade Convention permitted the unopposed advance of Serbian and Rumanian forces into Hungarian territory and a military occupation in accordance with The Hague Regulations, in other words, without replacing the existing civilian administration in the occupied territories. The general cessation of hostilities also made possible the crossing of the northwestern Hungarian frontiers by Czech troops. All told, three-fourths of defeated Hungary's territory and two-thirds of her population came under foreign military occupation between the autumn of 1918 and the spring of 1919. The Treaty of Trianon during the summer of 1920 was to turn occupation into annexation — with a significant exception.

This exception was Baranya and its county seat Pécs. The Serbian Army crossed the Drava River into Baranya on November 14, 1918; entered Pécs the same day; continued and penetrated north beyond the Belgrade Convention line; and went into permanent quarters for nearly three years south of the line of demarcation it had unilaterally established. Four-fifths of the county, including the city of Pécs, were thus detached from the mother country. The line of northernmost Yugoslav military penetration, separating the northern unoccupied one-fifth of Baranya from the southern Yugoslav-held four-fifths of the county, became stationary by January 1919 and ran westward from the Danube along a boundary north of the communes Dinnyeberki, Bükkösd, Megyefa, Bakonya, Kővágószöllös, Kővágótöttös, Magyarürög, Pécsbudafa, Hosszuhetény, Pécsvárad, Zengővárkony, Pusztakisfalu, and Apátvarasd.[4] East and north of the Danube, in the present Yugoslav Voyvodina, the Serbian Army stopped in its northward march at the Belgrade Convention line. Unlike in Baranya, east of the Danube there were no coal mines.

In Pécs, the maverick city, where conservative-radical contradictions had been kept in a precarious equilibrium by the Austro-Hungarian status quo, foreign military occupation added a new component to the political metabolism. The events which ensued were unique in the process which brought into existence the new Middle

Europe. The presence of foreign troops was unresistingly recognized by both the conservative Right and the radical Left as a safeguard preventing the opposing ideological camp from gaining the upper hand in county and city. All eyes were fixed on Budapest. A radical postwar government of the Left in that distant national capital (according to contemporary standards, but only 197 kilometers or 122 miles, as the crow flies) was powerless to extend its anti-rightist measures to occupied Baranya because of the Yugoslav military presence. Similarly, a conservative régime of the Right in the capital would not be able to move in a counterrevolutionary manner against the leftists ensconced in Pécs as long as they were protected by the armed forces of a victorious new state anxious to establish optimum national frontiers. The political situation in Pécs-Baranya during 1918-1921 evolved, therefore, in the form of three interlocked processes: the local tug-of-war between Right and Left; the governmental metamorphoses in Budapest from conservatism to bourgeois and then to proletarian radicalism, followed by an anti-red White Terror; and finally victorious Yugoslavia's maneuverings to achieve its maximum territorial aspirations at defeated Hungary's expense. The architects of the new Middle European status quo in Paris, however, were more concerned about the Soviet threat from the East than about Yugoslavia's new frontiers. The two problems had to be solved integrally, the new frontiers had to be drawn as functions of the continental anti-Bolshevik strategic plan. But the exuberant Yugoslav falcon kept in its wide gyre, unable to hear the calls of the Paris falconers.

3. *Effects of Defeat on Right and Left*

During the closing months of the first world war, under the impact of impending defeat, Hungary had begun moving leftward on the political spectrum. On October 31, 1918 Michael Károlyi (1875-1955), leader of the pro-Allied opposition, was named Prime Minister at the head of a coalition government composed of his personal followers, Bourgeois Radicals, and Social Democrats. Károlyi, who became President of the new Hungarian People's Republic on January 11, 1919, remained in power only until March 20, 1919. On that date he resigned with his whole government in protest against the Allied policy of ceding additional Hungarian territory to Rumania, another of the victorious small powers, which at that time was engaged in carrying out the supreme Allied policy by military intervention in south Russia. Rather than accept the diplomatic note permitting a further Rumanian military advance toward Hungary's interior, handed him on March 20 by French Lieutenant Colonel Ferdinand Vyx,[5] Károlyi resigned in the conviction that, his pro-Allied policy having failed, the only possible remaining Hungarian political orientation was toward Moscow. To effect this reorientation, he handed power to the Social Democrats, unaware that these had already agreed with the Communist leader Béla Kun (1886–1939) on an SDP-Communist Party (CPH) merger and on the proclamation of the dictatorship of the proletariat.[6] Due to this shift in government, Hungary became the westernmost outpost of Communism in the world.

At the same time, with the rise of the Hungarian Soviet Republic in March 1919, the secondary concern of making territorial arrangements in Middle Europe satisfactory to small allies, was surpassed in Paris and London by an anxiety of the first magnitude about erecting a mid-continental barrier to westward Soviet expansionism. Whereas before Béla Kun the Allies had simply favored the claims of friendly states — Czechoslovakia, the Serb-Croat-Slovene Kingdom, and Rumania — against a defeated Hungary too lately converted to the Allied cause, with Kun in power in Budapest, the French and the British proceeded to apply their anti-Bolshevik interventionist policy to Soviet Hungary.[7] The new states of Middle Europe had to be organized not only on the basis of victorious nationalism but also as a conservative bloc, a *cordon sanitaire,* to contain the continental spread of Soviet power and Communist ideology. Accordingly, after being assigned more Hungarian territory in the spring of 1919, during the ensuing summer the Rumanian Army received Allied approval to dislodge the Hungarian Soviets from Budapest. This was done. At the approach of the Rumanian invaders Béla Kun resigned on August 1, 1919 and handed power to a "Government of the Trade Unions," which lasted six days, at the end of which it was replaced on August 7 by a weak counterrevolutionary régime. Chaotic political conditions followed until a stronger combination of the counterrevolutionary Right, answering the requirements of the Allied *cordon sanitaire* containment policy, could be permitted to rise to power under the last Commander-in-Chief of the Austro-Hungarian Navy, Admiral Nicholas Horthy (1868–1957). On November 16, 1919 Horthy entered Budapest, evacuated on the previous day by Rumanian troops, at the head of the Hungarian National Army.

This was the new ultraconservative force holding power in unoccupied Hungary for the remainder of the interim period between the Belgrade Convention (November 13, 1918) and the Treaty of Peace (June 4, 1920). Actually the Horthy régime was to remain in power until it was demolished by Hitler's Nazis on October 16, 1944.

The advent of the Horthy régime in Hungary was welcomed in Baranya by the local Right with glee and damned with gloom by the countervailing Left, just as the brief rule of Béla Kun (March 21– August 1, 1919) had been jeered by the Baranya Right and cheered by its antithetic Left. It appeared that, in the case of the Hungarian population of the occupied county and city, nationalism during the Budapest gyrations imperceptibly assumed a position subordinate to class consciousness and interests. The occupying Yugoslav power, on the other hand, placed national interests above ideology. It played the role, first, of the protector of the local Right against the leftward-drifting régimes in Budapest. Later, it switched sides and became a defender of the local separatist Left against the new anti-Communist rulers in the unoccupied Hungarian center. In both cases the motivating force was Yugoslav nationalism, which had for its objective in Baranya a prolonged occupation and a possible eventual annexation of newly acquired coal-rich territories.

The final disposition of these interlocking interests of the Baranya Left and the South Slav nationalists was in Allied hands before the Great Power judicatories of the French capital. Recognition by the Great Powers in the peace treaty of the unauthorized, northernmost line of Serbian military penetration would have been tantamount to placing Yugoslav national aspirations above continental Allied strategy. Accepting the Belgrade Convention line as the new international frontier might have been interpreted as Allied indifference to the intrusion of Communism into Middle Europe. Enforcing the validity of a new treaty boundary between Hungary and Yugoslavia, south of both the line of demarcation and the Belgrade Convention boundary, was to serve notice to the new small states allied to the victors that national aspirations in Middle Europe must be weighed in the balance against acceptance of the overall *cordon sanitaire* policy. Given this postwar diplomatic climate, the effect of the Austro-Hungarian defeat on the Baranya Left was a fiasco of the party line. As far as the Baranya Right was concerned, the political effects of defeat were first manifested as a temporary eclipse on the provincial stage of history, soon ended by a recasting in the traditionally dominant role — even if only for the interwar quarter century.

III

Baranya and the Károlyi Régime: The Era of Undivided Loyalty

Two weeks elapsed between Michael Károlyi's coming to power in Budapest at the head of a predominantly bourgeois-democratic régime (October 31, 1918) and the entry of Yugoslav troops into Pécs (November 14, 1918). These two weeks were a period of revolutionary transition in Baranya as well as in the remainder of Hungary. Károlyi personally headed the delegation which went to sign the separate Hungarian Military Convention in Belgrade, permitting the entry of Serbian military units and the evacuation of designated Hungarian areas by Hungarian troops.[1] On November 16 the National Council ruling in Budapest proclaimed Hungary "a people's republic independent and separate from any other state."[2] A new country was born in Belgrade two weeks later, on December 1: the Kingdom of the Serbs, Croats, and Slovenes (SHS), the future (1929) Yugoslavia.[3] Chaotic conditions in the border areas accompanied the waxing of the new South Slav state and the waning of the old Hungarian kingdom.

A struggle against spreading political and economic anarchy characterized the first two weeks of November 1918 in Baranya. Following the example of Budapest, extralegal governmental organizations known as national councils[4] were established in the county and its communes. The first problems national councils had to deal with were those of public security: the looting of shops, warehouses, and freight trains; a pogrom-like outbreak of one day's duration in the town of Mohács; the eruption of long-smoldering animosities between large landowners and landless peasants; an evening of scores with unpopular officials of the fallen old régime; clashes in the southern part of the county between Slavic- and Hungarian-speaking villagers; and above all, the problem of supplying the population with food, if only to keep it from resorting to revolutionary excesses.[5] There was a surfeit of coal but no food in Baranya. To the south, across the Drava river in Croatia, the opposite was the case: food but no coal. The obvious answer was the organization of a barter of commodities, but such an exchange of goods depended on the security of the Pécs-Osijek rail-road line as well as on the inviolability of the factories, the warehouses, and the retail shops.[6]

The Pécs National Council attempted to solve the multitude of its problems by tackling security first.[7] The formation of a Citizens' Guard of volunteers was ordered. However, between November 1 and 4 only 400 men volunteered. This was a force insufficient even to ensure the safety of the industrial plants alone. By November 5 the Council had to resort to the organization in three key plants of a special corps of Factory Guards under the command of military officers. Still the looting continued, perpetrated mostly by disbanded returning soldiers and by the *Lumpenproletariat* of the city. To bring under some form of control the lawless, marauding veterans, the National Council undertook their incorporation into a Military Guard, of which two companies were ready by November 3. The Military Police was reorganized at the same time. Continuing disorder prompted the Ministry of War in Budapest to order at the end of the first week of November the establishment by conscription of a pro-vincial National Guard, which was to be placed under the command of the local Chief of Police and organizationally included in the frame-work of the local Police and Fire Departments. Four companies of the National Guard, plus a fifth company recruited exclusively from industrial workers, were in existence by November 15. In addition, a special Railroads National Guard had begun functioning during the first week of November. Its assigned tasks were the prevention of trouble at the depots and the guarding of rolling stock both at stations and while in motion. Soldiers returning by rail from the fighting fronts fallen silent were first disarmed at the train stops and then recruited into the Railroads National Guard on the promise of being fed and paid 25 crowns every day.[8]

The value of 25 crowns was hard to determine. There were two kinds of banknotes in circulation by mid-November: the so-called "blue money," old issues of the Austro-Hungarian Bank; and the unpopular "white money," newly issued and printed only on one side. If accepted (which was not always the case) "white money" was discounted by at least 25%. In Pécs there was neither blue nor white money in circula-tion during the first few days of the National Council,[9] which now had to face another difficult problem: how to pay the security personnel freshly organized to bring a semblance of normality out of spreading anarchy.

The problem was solved by placing a forced levy on the local

Savings Bank. One-half million crowns were paid into the Treasury of the Pécs National Council immediately; another million and a half by mid-November. The supplementary amount was placed at the Council's disposal by a hastily-summoned assembly of large landowners, major plant shareholders, and prosperous merchants. These men were pillars of the local Right, appealed to on the basis of patriotism.[10]

Conditions resembling normality were thus slowly returning to Pécs and Baranya when, in accordance with the Belgrade Convention of November 13, Serbian troops crossed the Drava river on the same day and entered Pécs on November 14. The limits of the occupation did not become firm for another six months, but after stabilization four-fifths of the county found itself under Yugoslav occupation. The unoccupied one-fifth, which continued to be governed by successive Budapest régimes, comprised only the county's northernmost Hegyhát (Sásd) district plus parts of three other districts (járás).[11]

The Serbian army unit which entered Pécs on November 14 consisted of 600 infantrymen and 100 cavalry under the command of 17 officers, the highest ranking of whom was a Lieutenant Colonel. Mayor Andor Nendtvich of Pécs, a conservative holdover from the old régime, spoke a few words of welcome at the suburban Üszög railroad station. The Serbian Commanding Officer replied by stating that he and his men had come as brothers. They would hold inviolate, he assured, the private property of individuals but would immediately proceed to sequester all military equipment and property.[12] During the ensuing days another Serbian military contingent detrained at the Pécs main railroad station and marched up Indóház-utca (now Szabadság Street) toward the center of the city, to the wonderment of children abandoning their games to flock to the sidewalks. They saw brave fighting men, under arms since 1914, who had retreated from their invaded country southward across the wild Albanian mountains to the island of Corfu, and thence sailed undaunted to the Salonika front to fight their way home north to the Danube. They were not the spit-and-polish soldiers of Austria-Hungary some of the children remembered seeing during the early, confident years of the war. These soldiers wore ill-fitting uniforms, leather sandals, and some of them rode muleback without sandals. This was a Balkan army, brave and victorious, but symbolic of the political Balkanization of Middle Europe then just beginning.

On November 15 the Serbian Commanding Officer made a courtesy call on Count-Bishop Zichy, whom he regarded as the highest dignitary in the occupied city. The Bishop did not fail to return the call a day later. Civil society could now go about its business under military protection, even if it was extended by another country. The situation, however, was strained. Pécs had not been under enemy occupation since the Revolution of 1848–49[13] and the presence of a strange soldiery in the city came as a shock. But law-abiding citizens consoled themselves by saying that, after all, the intrusion of the foreign army was only temporary and that, at least, one no longer had to worry about security of person and property.

Hopes of the latter category, however, proved to be ill-founded. Relations between the occupiers and the occupied began deteriorating almost immediately. Hungarians had an ingrained habit of considering Serbs political upstarts and cultural inferiors. Yet, at the same time, contempt was mixed with a certain amount of admiration for the manly virtues, especially military valor.[14] The Serbs were the Hungarians' favorite enemies. The invaders smarted under this qualified disdain, nor could they easily forget the four years of military depredations their country had suffered under Austro-Hungarian military occupation from 1914 to 1918. Photographs showing Austro-Hungarian officers in the act of hanging Serb *franc-tireurs* during the early days of the war, made their appearance briefly in the windows of a hat shop owned by a Yugoslav sympathizer in Király-utca. The vanquished of 1914 had now entered as victors the land of their former conquerors.

In the intoxication of triumph the Serbs chose to ignore the pertinent paragraphs of the Belgrade Convention, by which they were bound, and those of The Hague Regulations governing military occupation, by which they were not. The Hague Regulations specified that the occupying military power must leave intact the existing organs of civilian government and that it was to respect — except in the event of absolute hindrance *(empêchement)* — the laws in force of the occupied territory (Annex, Article XLIII).[15] This could be considered as irrelevant by the occupiers because Serbia (and its successor the SHS Kingdom) had not ratified any of The Hague Conventions.[15a] Article I of the Belgrade Military Convention, to which Serbia was a signatory, did however state that Hungarian civilian administration was to continue in occupied Hungarian territories.[16] As the occupation began in the autumn of 1918 there was no apparent Yugoslav interference with Hungarian local government.[17] By February 1919, however, the occupiers began establishing an illegal civilian administration. They also introduced the Yugoslav legal system, with the laws of the SHS Kingdom equally applied in territories to be annexed and in areas only occupied.[18] The Serb thinking behind this was that all territories occupied would be annexed, whereas the Hungarians hoped that most of the areas occupied would escape annexation. The administrative irritant was made worse by the facts that the Yugoslav civilians introduced into the Baranya local government were mostly Croatians and Bachka Serbs[19] — former Hungarian subjects who had a tendency to be chauvinistic — and that, as time went on, remaining Hungarian civil servants were required to take an oath to the King of Yugoslavia.[20] There was also divided authority among the occupiers. The Yugoslav military on Hungarian soil took their orders from the Belgrade General Staff in the SHS Ministry of War, while the civilian functionaries were employees of the newly-organized BBB Section (Bachka, Banat, Baranya) of the SHS Ministry of the Interior.[21] At times the civilian and military areas of authority overlapped. In the light of the foregoing the Hungarians were not entirely without legal grounds in beginning to claim, hopelessly, of course, that Yugoslav military authority in Baranya — the only legal occupational authority recognized by international law — became nonexistent as soon as the occupiers resorted to the organization of an impermissible parallel civilian administration.[22] At the time, however, in the twilight zone between war and peace, this was merely legalistic quibbling, with no court of international justice ready to hear the complaint.

The fault did not lie exclusively with the occupying Serbs. Occupying armies seldom, if ever, succeed in endearing themselves to occupied populations. Trouble on a small scale began in Pécs during the early winter of 1918–19, when the reported custom of Serb soldiers to leave shops without paying for their purchases was first generally noticed.[23] Then came arbitrary military requisitioning of industrial and personal property on orders from the Yugoslav military command. This was no longer just a lack of discipline. The local press was then placed under Yugoslav military censorship. Public warehouses were forcibly emptied. The local authorities were prevented from collecting taxes. The movement of goods by rail was reduced to a trickle, so that neither raw materials could reach the plants nor finished goods could be transported toward their normal marketing outlets in unoccupied Hungary. The city soon plunged into an economic depression marked by inflation as well as unemployment.[24] The Yugoslav employees of the Belgrade BBB Section, who began infiltrating the local administration, were paid in dinars, which had no fixed rate of exchange for either Hungarian "blue" or "white money." A bewildering variety of currencies — dinars, SHS crowns, stamped crowns, unstamped blue money, unstamped white money — were freely floating on the market.[25] Gradually it became apparent that the occupiers were primarily interested not in complying with the provisions of The Hague Regulations but in two nationalistic objectives of their own: (1) exploitation of the Pécs coal mines to the fullest, immediately; and (2) annexing the whole occupied area, eventually. One of the ways to attain the first goal was to ban all miners' unions and to place the miners under Serbian military jurisdiction. To prepare for the second objective, eventual annexation, the occupied territory was subjected to measures of economic reorientation, which included weaning it to the *dinar* area financially and making it dependent on Yugoslavia both for raw materials and marketing outlets.

Portent of Yugoslav imperialistic intentions came from Belgrade on December 1, 1918 in the form of a governmental announcement to the effect that the SHS Kingdom would permanently annex the occupied Hungarian areas of Bachka, Banat, and Baranya.[26] The announcement was followed by a gradual changing of place names on official buildings — railroad stations, courthouses — in southern Baranya villages from Hungarian to Serbo-Croatian and from the Latin to the Cyrillic script. Parallel with these overt activities went covert Pan-Yugoslav propaganda, spread mostly in the countryside but also in Pécs, by agents extolling for the population the advantages of transferring Baranya from allegiance to a defeated country to the sovereignty of a victorious state, ally of the Great Powers. In January 1919 there was a painful flag incident in Pécs. An exuberantly patriotic Hungarian youth climbed the tower of the City Hall and replaced the Yugoslav flag with a Hungarian tricolor.[27] The Hungarian colors were thereupon hauled down by the Yugoslav soldiery, dragged and trampled upon in the mud in the sight of a quickly-gathered crowd of shocked curiosity seekers. News of the senseless outrage to patriotic sentiments quickly spread through the city, kindling sullen hatred among the population against the occupiers.

The flag incident brought into sharp focus the issue of territorial sovereignty. To most inhabitants of Pécs a change of sovereignty was inconceivable. Historical memories were stored with a past of a nearly one thousand years of Hungarian statehood. The first shock of the December 1918 Belgrade declaration of intention to annex Baranya was felt by both Left and Right in the occupied county and in the polarized city of Pécs. For the Left all reservations of loyalty to the Hungarian center had disappeared with the fall of the old régime and by the Socialist-supported republican transformation. For the Right historic loyalties to the governing national authority had not been weakened, in the beginning, by a change in the form of government from monarchy to a bourgeois republic. Not all men of the Right were monarchists; some of them were in fact flagbearers of the concept of national independence last fought for in 1848–49. Right and Left therefore reacted to the Belgrade annexionist declaration of December 1 by proclaiming their undivided loyalty to the Hungarian People's Republic.

This expression of Hungarian nationalism, though not necessarily of republicanism, took the form of a "People's Resolution"[28] passed and published by a grand assembly of the inhabitants of Pécs on December 3, 1918. In its preamble the document rejected the assumption that "this city [of Pécs], a change in whose appurtenance has never been moot since the age of migrations, might be detached from the territory of Hungary and joined either to a Greater Serbia or to any other state structure." The People's Resolution then went on to stress that "even today Pécs is a city belonging to the Hungarian People's Republic which wants to remain such under any and all conditions." The document stressed that the people of Pécs "protest all endeavors which would attempt to tear [their] city from Hungary" and ended on the high patriotic note: "We were Hungarians, are Hungarians, and want to remain citizens of the Hungarian People's Republic."[29]

Here was nationalism unmitigated by any other ideology; undivided loyalty to the mother country above parties and factions. The signatories of the Resolution included not only the members of the National Council and of the Pécs Municipality but also of representatives of all political parties (Independence, Radical, Christian Socialist, and Social Democratic), all major religious denominations (Roman Catholic, Lutheran, Reformed, and Israelite), all social organizations (National Casino, Citizens' Casino, Catholic Circle, Masonic Lodge, and Feminists' Association), as well as most lately-sprung revolutionary organizations ("councils" of workers, artisans, railroad workers, mailmen, etc.), in addition to the Chamber of Commerce and Industry, the Association of Manufacturers, and the Merchants' Club.[30]

The following day principal signers of the Resolution were arrested by the Yugoslav Border Police (a Belgrade Ministry of Interior organ) and kept jailed for four days. This was meant apparently as a warning to check the growing resistance to the occupiers. The resistance movement was spearheaded by the SDP and its unions, in cooperation with the CSP, and efficiently assisted by the illegal CPH. The latter disposed of several underground cells among intellectuals and, most opportunely, among the communications workers of the Hungarian State Railways (MÁV).[31] At the same time, in spite of the CSP presence in the still inactive resistance, a certain degree of rapprochement was noticeable between the occupiers and the high conservative circles of the Right.

This was a corollary of the increasing apprehension with which the Baranya *beati possidentes* followed the nationalizing attitudes and intentions of the Károlyi régime in unoccupied Hungary. On January 1, 1919 the Salgótarján mines in the north were seized by the miners[32] with little resistance from the Hungarian authorities. Indeed, the Budapest official gazette announced that by the end of March 1919 all mines in the country would be placed under the Ministry of Commerce as a first step toward nationalization.[33] Land reform aimed at the elimination of oversize landed property was another avowed aim of the Károlyi régime. "People's Law" XVIII, voted on February 16, 1919, forecast the distribution of all landed estates over 500 *holds* (one Hungarian *hold* equals 1.42 acres) among the landless agricultural population.[34] Even before the law could go into effect, the high-minded Károlyi began on February 23, 1919 to distribute his own landed estates among his incredulous peasants.[35] Reunion with the mother country at the end of the Yugoslav occupation would certainly mean the extension of the nationalization laws into Baranya, across the line of demarcation. The leftward drift in Budapest now was turning this purely military frontier into an ideological boundary between socialism and private enterprise. The Baranya mines and the large estates, including those of the Diocese and the Chapter were at stake. They would remain intact, beyond the reach of a nationalizing government only as long as the Yugoslav Army continued to hold back the tide at the ideological boundary north of the Mecsek massif. The changing attitudes of the Right could be conjectured by the improving relations between Count-Bishop Zichy, the highest acknowledged dignitary of the city, and the top stratum of the occupiers. In the beginning these relations were formally protocolary; now they were becoming warmly social. At receptions given in the episcopal palace the Count-Bishop provided social occasions for the top Yugoslav military and civilians to meet leading industrialists of the city. Hunts were organized on the large landed estates of the occupied county to allow fraternization between the local Hungarian gentry and ranking Yugoslav potentates.[36] The fear of socialism was making inroads into the intensity of traditional nationalism.

Not unexpectedly the rapprochement between the Right and the occupiers was accompanied by an estrangement between the Left and the Yugoslav rulers. The growing alienation of the latter two was only a prelude to the bitter struggle which was looming up between the Serbian military and the Pécs miners. Invaluable assistance was rendered to the miners by the legal Socialists and the still illegal Communists in MÁV (Hungarian State Railroads)[37] employ. Growing unemployment, inflation, and the unavailability of food helped spread the popular discontent seething in Baranya to Yugoslav-occupied areas east of the Danube. SDP organizations in this territory, especially in the cities of Szabadka (Subotica) and Temesvár (Timisoara), became centers of resistance. Late in February 1919 Socialist delegates from these two occupied towns agreed with the leaders of the Pécs workers and miners that the proper reply to the arbitrariness of the Serbs was a general strike. Since organizationally Szabadka (Subotica) was the weakest link in the conspiratorial chain, it was decided that Szabadka would give the prearranged, coded signal with the help of MÁV railroad communications workers organized in secret Communist cells, for the simultaneous beginning of the general strike through the whole Yugoslav-occupied area.[38]

The coded signal was received in Pécs from Szabadka through MÁV telegraphic facilities on February 21, 1919.[39] At once a 42-member delegation, including workers' and miners' union leaders, called upon the Yugoslav commanding officer in Pécs with a memorandum containing the following demands:

Improvements in transportation to and from unoccupied Hungary; in provisioning the city of Pécs; in making available raw materials to industrial plants; currency reform; permission for union activity; removal of Yugoslav functionaries from local government; and a complete restoration of Hungarian civil administration.[40]

The reply of the Yugoslav commanding officer to these demands was to place the members of the delegation under arrest and have nine of them deported for internment in the Serbian town of Mitrovica. The nine were to be considered as hostages. Orders were issued which were to be complied with immediately: resumption of work wherever it had stopped, a state of siege, and a curfew in the city from 7 p.m. to 6 a.m.[41] In spite of these Draconic measures, however, the general strike was complete in all factories, workshops, railroad and streetcar lines; post, telephone and telegraph facilities (the telephone lines were sabotaged), gasworks, mines, offices, schools, newspapers, and retail stores. In Pécs and environs alone, about 15,000 workers and miners went on strike. Attempts to force the miners to descend into the shafts under Yugoslav military guard were of no avail. The only result was the flight of resisting miners into the mountains and woods, and across the line of demarcation into unoccupied Hungarian territory. By early March only electricity and the pumping system of the mines were working in and around Pécs.

At this point the occupying authorities decided to starve the strikers into submission. Price controls on groceries and meats were suspended. Yugoslav military patrols met villagers on their way to the Pécs market places and confiscated the produce they were bringing with them. All meetings involving more than four persons were prohibited. Wives of strikers were taken away as hostages and sent to forced labor. Serbian cavalry charged and beat with the flat of the sword demonstrators in the streets. Sympathy demonstrations took place in Yugoslavia, where Serbian Socialists especially became vociferous in protesting the use of their military as Cossacks in Pécs.

After eighteen days the desperate Yugoslav need for coal decided the outcome of the general strike. Colonel Radovanovitch, the rough-and-ready Yugoslav commanding officer in Pécs, was replaced by the urbane Colonel Cholak-Antitch, a former Serbian Military Attaché in Paris. A preliminary agreement with Cholak-Antitch in Pécs, followed by a final settlement on March 18, 1919 with the Deputy Chief of Staff of the SHS Army in Belgrade, brought the general strike to an end. The occupiers granted, in return for the "loyal comportment of the Hungarian inhabitants of Pécs and continued work in the mines,"[42] the following demands of the strikers:

No more removal of food from Pécs and Baranya; factories to be supplied with raw materials and marketing facilities; untrammeled resumption of the movement of persons and goods; no interference with the PTT (post, telegraph and telephone) services; first priority for Pécs and Baranya needs from the yield of the Pécs mines; unemployment compensation; no further dismissals of Hungarian administrative functionaries; release of all arrested strikers; undisturbed activity for the trade unions; abolition of the censorship of the press; reinstatement of dismissed Hungarian civil administrators; and gradual recall of all Yugoslav personnel from local government.[43]

It was a famous victory for the Socialist workers of Baranya loyal to their homeland. But the high patriotic note of the December 3, 1918 People's Resolution was missing from the SDP proclamation of March 13, 1919 which announced the end of the general strike to the inhabitants of Pécs. The only reason the proclamation gave for beginning and fighting the strike to a victorious finish was the workers' determination to end "economic misery."[44] Thus economics was clearly discernible in the ideological and political motivation of both Right and Left by the end of the first phase of the occupation. The haves of the Right were reluctant to sacrifice their property on the altar of nationalism. The have-nots of the Left had no such choice to make but were still willing to strike a blow for their country's sovereignty while fighting to improve their economic condition.

As soon as the curtain fell on the first act, it was ready to rise on the second. Two days after the end of the general strike in Baranya the bourgeois-democratic régime of Michael Károlyi collapsed in Budapest and was replaced by a Hungarian Soviet Republic dominated by Béla Kun. The assumption of power by the revolutionary proletariat in the political center was a deathblow to undivided national loyalties in peripheral Baranya. The Right and Left now took up new positions: the former at a discreet distance from nationalism; the latter fusing with it in a passionate embrace.

IV

Baranya and the Béla Kun Régime:
The Period of Proletarian Nationalism

The rise of the Hungarian Soviet Republic (HSR) in unoccupied
territory acted in Baranya as an ideological inhibitor on the Right and
as a catalyst speeding up the amalgam of socialism and nationalism for
the Left. The interests of the Right required and its comportment
indicated that, until the return to a rightist political course in the
center, Baranya had better remain under foreign military occupation,
temporarily detached from the Communist-controlled mother country. As for the Left, never before had the Baranya workers and miners
beén more attached in allegiance to the national capital of their
country than now, with the revolutionary proletariat in power in
Budapest. A bewildered American observer in that city described the
new ideological configuration produced by the Magyars as "an un-
natural alliance of nationalism and socialism."[1]

There is no evidence to indicate an immediate retreat of the Baranya
Right from the pursuit of nationalistic goals. As elsewhere in Hungary,
the initial conservative reaction to Béla Kun's rise to power was
watchful waiting and even occasional endorsement of the "new
order."[2] The foreign policy of the HSR revived nationalist hopes for
territorial integrity; indeed, the new régime was swept into power on a
"tidal wave of nationalist sentiment," which caused the ruling Left to
consider itself in possession of a "nationalist mandate."[2a] For a
fleeting moment in the spring of 1919 rightist nationalism was
apparently fusible with socialism in its most radical form, provided
that socialism should serve nationalistic objectives. Some Hungarians
and foreigners looked on turning toward Moscow as a nationalist
protest.[3] But ideological fusibility was quickly dissipated for the Right
by the plethora of socializing decrees issued by the Hungarian Soviets
between March 26 and April 3. Industrial plants, mines, transportation, medium-size and large landed estates, as well as educational
institutions became socialist property within a week.[4]

All non-proletarian, propertied interests were psychologically affected in occupied Baranya. In the unoccupied Hegyhát (Sásd) district *(járás)*, landed estates were being turned into collectives. The Christian Socialist Party of Pécs (CSP) officially announced its acceptance of collectivization.[5] But the CSP did not speak for the prosperous middle-peasants, the gentry, the aristocratic landowners, and the plant and mine shareholders and directors, who were now united for the 133-day duration of the Hungarian Soviets in one common purpose: the national center must not impose its Communist system on occupied Baranya. Counterrevolutionary stirrings in the unoccupied parts of neighboring Somogy County[6] were watched with sympathy. When, in mid-May 1919, a Yugoslav-sponsored local interest group was dispatched to lobby at the peace conference in Paris under the Belgrade-appointed Yugoslav Prefect Pandurovitch, it is said to have included two great Hungarian landowners, Counts Paul Keglevich and Ivan Draskovich, in addition to the leading Baranya jurist Tivadar Andrits, a former member of the Hungarian Parliament.[7] According to a surviving Socialist observer of the 1919 scene in Baranya, some local conservatives were at such low ebb of their nationalism at that time that they were considering union of their occupied county area with Yugoslavia.[8]

At the other end of the Baranya political spectrum, the amalgam of socialism and nationalism was facilitated by economic factors. Wages were higher in HSR territory than in Pécs and its environs. First a trickle and then a torrent of Pécs-Baranya workers and miners began to flow northward across the line of demarcation into Soviet Hungary. Within a few weeks in April–May enough Baranya proletarians fled north not only to provide a surfeit of industrial labor but also to fill seven battalions of the newly organized Hungarian Red Army.[9] The example of rank-and-file proletarians was followed by their leaders. Ten of the Pécs Socialist chiefs transferred their activities to the HSR-controlled parts of neighboring Somogy County. From there they established direct contact with Béla Kun in Budapest.[10] They also set up a command post for political, military and propaganda purposes. Propaganda was directed toward Pécs by every available means, including leaflet-dropping military planes[11] bombarding the population with appeals to support the Socialist fatherland. Beyond the range of surplus World War I planes, special Serbo-Croatian speaking agents crossed to the south bank of the Drava River to revolutionize the South-Slav inhabitants. Contact was claimed to have been established not only with the Communist Party of Yugoslavia (which was thought to be anxious to have the Hungarian Red Army attack the

SHS Kingdom and help establish a Soviet republic in its place)[12] but also with the radical Croatian peasant leader Stephan Radich,[13] who appeared to be more interested in an independent Croatia than in a centralized Yugoslav state. French colonial troops south of the Drava were also chosen as a propaganda target group, but the linguistic barrier prevented progress on this sector.[14]

During and after the successful offensive of the Hungarian Red Army in the late spring of 1919 against the Czechoslovak occupation forces in the north, the Baranya refugees in Somogy County began concentrating their energies on preparing the people of Baranya for what they thought would be a quick military re-occupation by the Hungarians.[15] In a letter addressed to Béla Kun and also in personal conversations,[16] Julius Hajdu, the most prominent Baranya Socialist leader in exile, proposed and pressed for the entry of HSR military forces into Yugoslav-occupied Baranya.[17] But Kun showed strategic acumen in rejecting the proposal. The HSR, he explained, was already fighting, with limited resources, on two fronts: against the Czechoslovaks in the north and the invading Rumanians in the east. Opening a third front in the south against the Yugoslavs was beyond the military capabilities of the Hungarian Red Army and against the interests of the HSR.[18] The Kun-Hajdu exchange remained personal and unpublicized. Publicly Béla Kun kept the Yugoslavs on their toes by refusing to recognize the line of demarcation established by their army, even where it coincided with the Belgrade Convention boundary.[19] Thus the Baranya front remained nervously quiet and pacific during the brief life-span of the HSR.

While the nationalism of the Baranya Left was waxing to chauvinism, the economic situation in Pécs was not developing to the liking of the occupiers. A new and disturbing factor entered into the pre-eminent Yugoslav occupation problem, which was maintaining coal production at a maximum level. After the proclamation of the dictatorship of the proletariat in Budapest, a steady drop in the yield of the coalfields began owing to the northward flight of the Pécs miners to HSR territory.[20] Production was reduced perhaps to as low as one-third of the peacetime yield[21] not only because some of the miners had fled to unoccupied territory but also due to slowdowns in the shafts by the stay-homes. (The local term for slowdown was *amerikázás,* "work American style.")[22] The reduced yield of coal had to suffice both Yugoslav needs and local requirements. The acute demand for coal in HSR territory was ignored. In fact, after March 21, 1919, all north-bound coal shipments into Hungary proper were banned. Local coal

distribution in occupied Baranya was severely rationed. But there were
no cuts in the southbound shipments of coal on the rails of the Pécs-
Osijek trunkline across the Drava into Yugoslav territory. To maintain the undiminished deliveries to the homeland, the occupiers
brought pressure on the mine management to provide wage raises for
miners still at work.

One salutary result of the northward migration of workers and
miners was a sharp drop in Pécs unemployment and a corresponding
easing of socio-economic tensions. Since the general strike of March
1919 the occupying power had been doing its best to help the industrial
sector in Pécs by supplying it with raw materials from the Balkans and
by opening new markets for finished products in the SHS Kingdom.[23]
In so doing the Yugoslavs were not only keeping Pécs industries alive
but were also furthering their ulterior political objective, the reorientation of area economy toward Yugoslavia with a view to eventual
annexation. Such a solution of the occupation problem would not
have been altogether displeasing in the South-Slav populated villages
in the southeastern corner of the county, but it did tend to increase the
animosity of the Hungarian peasantry in the countryside toward Serb-
coddled "red" Pécs. The number of peasant women bringing produce
to the Pécs marketplaces started falling menacingly, without any
preventive interference by Yugoslav military patrols, as had been the
case during the 1919 general strike. The provisioning situation was
deteriorating toward a disaster. There were now more jobs to be had in
Pécs, but also a scarcity to feed hungry mouths.

All this undoubtedly had an effect on the visibly continuing
rapprochement between the Yugoslav occupiers and the Baranya
Right, which was paralleled by a growing estrangement between the
Serbs and the local Left. Within two weeks of the Hungarian Soviets'
coming to power in Budapest, the Yugoslav occupying authorities in
Baranya permitted the return to Pécs of its old-régime Mayor Andor
Nendtvich, whom they had expelled from their territories on January
30, 1919, during the period of still undivided Right-Left loyalty to the
center. Since by late spring the Pécs press had become predominantly
leftist (the bourgeois-liberal daily *Pécsi Napló* was taken over by the
trade unions in mid-April),[24] military censorship was made more
severe.[25] The celebration of International Labor Day on May 1, 1919
was banned. Relations between the SHS and the HSR remained
strained during the entire brief existence of the latter and cast their
shadow over the local scene.

While the Béla Kun régime lasted in Budapest, the Yugoslav stance was characterized by distrust toward Kun's Baranya supporters and by a sense of strategic insecurity. Avoiding anything that might be taken as provocation, every effort was made to strengthen Yugoslav defenses against a possible attack by the Hungarian Soviets. Immediately after the Kun takeover in Budapest, Prince Regent Alexander of Yugoslavia asked General Franchet d'Esperey, commanding on the Balkan front, to transmit his request to Marshal Foch, the Supreme Allied Commander, for raising the effectives of the SHS Army to 250,000[26] men from an existing number of 100,000–120,000.[27] Simultaneously Belgrade began reinforcing its defensive positions both east and west of the Danube. In the village of Bisse, and probably also in other occupied rural communes, anti-Communist farmers grouped in Hunters' Clubs got back the shotguns they had to surrender at the beginning of the occupation.[28] Implementation of the Belgrade Convention provisions regarding the occupation was suspended. While taking these precautionary measures, however, Belgrade scrupulously avoided joining with Bucharest and Prague in military action against Soviet Hungary. In fact, the SHS Government gave notice to Rumania and Czechoslovakia, as early as April 1919, of its non-belligerent intentions toward Hungary. The French military observer in Baranya reported to his superiors that the Yugoslavs apparently hoped to turn the political situation in Hungary to their advantage in the belief that the Great Powers would not dare order a Yugoslav evacuation of Baranya and the other occupied territories because of the Bolshevik danger threatening from Béla Kun's Hungary.[29] Indeed, the Great Powers at this point were weighing the pros and cons of a military intervention in Hungary with the aid of Allied troops on the scene. The Yugoslavs were pressured to participate in a planned overthrow of the Kun régime, and they reluctantly agreed. On July 11, 1919 in Paris they apparently committed one division to march with six Rumanian, two French, and possibly one Czech divisions against Budapest,[30] and on July 17 Marshal Foch informed the heads of the Allied delegations in the French capital that the interallied forces of intervention in Hungary would include "18 to 20,000 excellent [Yugoslav] soldiers."[31] The plan never materialized, except for the offensive of the Rumanian Army which did reach Budapest during the first week of August 1919.

In Baranya the Yugoslavs dug in for the duration, then unforeseen, of the Hungarian Soviets, and did their best to prepare for a prolonged and permanent stay with the aid of two incongruous population groups. The first of these groups consisted of the anti-Communist

Hungarian landowning upper- and urban middle classes. The second population group comprised the Belgrade-oriented South-Slav peasantry, densely settled on the north side of the natural frontiers between Magyars and Serbs. Propaganda directed by the *Narodna Uprava*[32] (National Council) in Novi Sad, the administrative center of Yugoslav-occupied (and eventually annexed) Bachka (now Voyvodina), became active in Pécs, especially among Hungarian-speaking families with Bosnian surnames, historical leftovers from the Turkish wars of the fifteenth to the eighteenth centuries. Petitions, addressed to Belgrade, were circulated among this population stratum, asking for the annexation of Pécs and occupied Baranya to Yugoslavia.[33] In rural areas inhabited by a Serbo-Croatian-speaking peasantry, whether spontaneously or in an inspired manner, the villagers began demonstrating for Yugoslavia. In folk festivals held to celebrate the change in their place names from Hungarian to Serbo-Croatian, picturesquely dressed Slav rustics group-danced the Serbian *kolo* along the roadsides.

Amidst these ethnic rejoicings in the countryside, in the course of continuing Serb-Right rapprochement and Serb-Left estrangement in the urban areas, word came from the north during the first days of August that the Hungarian Soviets had fallen in Budapest. Hungary, its capital under Rumanian occupation, was in a state of anarchy in which counterrevolutionary, anti-Communist, nationalist forces were grouping and regrouping to fill the political vacuum. Once more the signal was given in the center for the peripheral Right and Left to shift positions on nationalism.

V

Baranya and the Horthy Régime: The Return to Bourgeois Nationalism

With the shift in power in the distant northern national center, a new change of partners was in order for the Baranya political cotillion. The Yugoslavs now withdrew from their flirts on the Right and tripped toward dancers recently distant on the Left. The basic rule of the ballet, pairing with a partner facing away from the center, was obeyed. The new partner moving in a centrifugal direction was the Left, for which proletarian internationalism became the style after August 1919. Union with the mother country, so earnestly desired while that parent wore a red garb, now was passionately rejected in favor of detachment, autonomy, or even annexation. It was more than simple political animosity of Left against Right. Refugees — radical, socialist, and communist — arriving from the north either directly or via Vienna, told terrifying tales of the White Terror raging in unoccupied territory.[1] A historically well-identified phenomenon stretching back to the French Revolution, the White Terror was the bloody revenge by extremist elements of the restored Right against a briefly-ruling Left fallen from power. In the Hungarian center of 1919–1920 the White Terror included the sadistic anti-Communist and anti-Semitic excesses of unruly officers' detachments as well as the politically-colored verdicts of an ultra-conservative judiciary. Now it was the Left instead of the Right which set itself against the extension into occupied Baranya of excesses committed by its opponent.

For the Baranya Right the disappearance in the center of the leftist inhibitor allowed a return to an old-fashioned, traditional nationalism. Henceforth it was the Right which wanted the Yugoslavs to leave and the Left which was anxious to have them stay. Additionally, the Left was being pushed farther toward its ideological extreme, first, by the political influence of Béla Kun's followers arriving from unoccupied territory;[2] and, second, by the increasing likelihood of Baranya's reincorporation in a Hungary convulsed by the White Terror. Wishful group-thinking is not an unknown political phenomenon at such junctures in history. During the summer of 1919, with its fortunes at their lowest ebb, the Hungarian Left lapsed into an unrealistic appraisal of seeming Soviet Russian gains at Allied expense. The Communist millennium appeared to be dawning. Conversely, the Right was not slow in developing a panicked empathy with the Allied Powers, a Great Fear of an impending Bolshevik breakthrough to the west.

While the flux of ideologies, the change of political partners, and the forming of new strategic configurations continued in the Baranya microcosm, and while Belgrade and Budapest were diplomatically vying for this small piece of land in the chancelleries of the Great Powers, in the minds of the Paris peacemakers the minor territorial dispute between Hungary and Yugoslavia assumed a certain relevance to the seeming westward surge of Bolshevism. The groundwork for the Hungarian peace treaty and for the new, restricted Hungarian frontiers was being laid during an international red scare marked by a Spartacist uprising in Berlin (January 1919), the establishment of the Third or Communist International (Comintern) in Moscow (March 2, 1919), the reality of the Hungarian Soviets (March–August 1919), the brief spectacle of a Soviet Republic in Bavaria (April–May 1919), a mutiny at Odessa in the French Black Sea fleet (April 16–22, 1919), the final failure of Allied intervention in revolutionary Russia both via Murmansk-Archangel (October 1919) and, almost simultaneously, in the southern Ukraine. The text of the Hungarian treaty was put in its final shape (January 15–May 4, 1920) in a psychological climate affected by another Spartacist insurrection, this time in the Ruhr (March 1920), and by the outbreak of a Polish-Russian war (April 25, 1920). The need for a Middle-European barrier against Communism seemed greater and more urgent than ever. Rumania was proving itself staunchly anti-Bolshevik by its war against the Soviets (May 18, 1919–March 2, 1920); the abortive Soviet republics in Slovakia (Bratislava in December 1918 and Preshov in June 1919) were things of the past. Only Yugoslavia, because of its sponsorship of a red régime in Baranya, appeared to be an unsealed spillway in the dam being built against Soviet political and ideological expansion. Were the Yugoslavs really so blind to the Bolshevik menace, asked Paris, that they would act as protectors of a Communist régime in the heart of Europe? Just to be able to push their boundaries a few miles farther north? Fact-finding Allied missions under American Lieutenant Colonel John B. Moore (November–December 1919) and under British Colonel Josiah Wedgwood, a former Laborite M.P. (June 1920), were dispatched to Baranya and to Hungary proper. An Interallied Military Commission (IMC), consisting of three French, British and Italian officers, was established in Pécs (May 28, 1920). Most indefatigable of the Allied military factfinders was the French Major Raoul Dérain, who arrived in Pécs in the spring of 1920 and quickly became the eyes and ears of Paris in the occupied city.

The complexities and intricacies of international politics facing the Great Powers in 1920 seemed to be lost on the Yugoslavs, except at home, where the growth of Communism was threatening the domestic status quo. Newly elected Communist municipal councils were dissolved in Belgrade in January 1920. In occupied Baranya, however, even a Comintern-affiliated régime was deemed deserving of protection and sponsorship as long as it served Yugoslav territorial and economic interests. Indeed, throughout the entire duration of the Yugoslav occupation in Baranya, the immutable policy of Belgrade was to seek an alliance with local population elements hostile to whatever government may be holding power in Budapest. Ideology, Right or Left, did not matter. The policy lines of the Great Powers did not count. The only concern was the furtherance of regional Yugoslav interests. Even ex-associates of Béla Kun, fleeing to Pécs for their lives after August 1, 1919, were hospitably received and politically utilized by the representatives of the Yugoslav Government, which was cracking down on its Communists at home. The Belgrade Ministry of Interior instructed its senior Pécs representative in September 1920 "to assimilate Hungarian political émigrés to the Hungarian [military] deserters."[3] This meant being placed under temporary police surveillance and then granted full political rights. The reports of the IMC to Paris via Budapest indicate that approximately 800 Hungarian Communist and affiliated political refugees arrived in Pécs via Vienna during the late summer of 1919.[4] After Yugoslav clearance, several of them (Dr. Geley, Steinmetz, Friedman, Lépes, Spolár, Szemennei, Váradi, Pál, Burger, Gállosi, Krausz, and Jelenszky) were reported to have become members of the governing Pécs Municipal Council.[5] In Major Dérain's opinion these men were "future troublemakers . . . who may compromise peace and quiet when the occupied territories are returned to Hungary."[6]

From the Yugoslav point of view the newcomers were reinforcements to assist in the conduct of Yugoslav policy in Baranya which, after the entrenchment of the Horthy régime in unoccupied territory, was aimed at (1) outmaneuvering the Budapest-oriented Right through ever-closer cooperation with the Left; (2) promoting support among all susceptible population elements for prolonged ties with Yugoslavia; and (3) maintaining and increasing coal deliveries to south of the Drava. This last objective had the most urgent priority. Consequently, the Yugoslav authorities readily allowed the return to occupied territory of the miners who had fled north during the Béla Kun régime to serve in the Hungarian Red Army.[7] To make sure, however, that the repatriates were not lying down on the job in the depths of the shafts and that the yield of coal was indeed on the upgrade, a Yugoslav Mining Commissioner was appointed with supreme supervisory powers. In the meantime, the propaganda effort to promote lasting ties with Yugoslavia was being extended from ethnically susceptible elements to the very heart of the Pécs labor movement. One way of winning friends and influencing people in this target group was to side with the workers in their wage fights with the DGHT-controlled mine management. Unprecedented concessions were made in this respect to the leftward-drifting labor unions in an effort which also served the political objective of outmaneuvering the Right with the aid of the Left.

The occupation continued to disregard the administrative clauses of the Belgrade Military Convention. Yugoslav control was retained and reinforced over the partly still Hungarian-staffed local government.[8] However, the new twist in policy called for new men at the top. Colonel Vuichitch was replaced as Commanding Officer of the occupation forces by Colonel Georgevitch; Prefect Pandurovitch (who was an ex-officer of the Austro-Hungarian Army and a former professor in a Pécs military high school), by the Bachka Serb Rayitch. Colonel Cholak-Antitch was brought back from Paris to lend his diplomatic finesse to the intricately evolving Baranya situation.[9] Under the new team censorship of the press became more stringent, with special reference to news from Budapest and from other European capitals.[10]

The local Left now found itself in the ambivalent position of being pampered by foreign occupiers and harassed by compatriot-employers. Specific instances of this ambivalence were the firing first of seventy, then 34, and later only 27 radical miners by the mine management.[11] The gradual decrease in the numbers dismissed was brought about by the intervention of the Yugoslav Mining Commissioner.[12] When, at the end of 1919 the management lowered wages to one-fifth of their prewar level (while increasing the price of coal twenty-fold over the peacetime average), the occupation authorities rammed through, in January 1920, a 30% hike in wages for both miners and industrial workers.[13] This wasn't, however, just manna from heaven for the employees, who had to conduct a series of slowdowns and strikes, which continued during the first half of 1920, to bring the employers to terms.[14] The occupiers kept on wooing the workers by such economic measures as placing controls on skyrocketing prices (by early 1920 meat, flour, and lard were available in Pécs only on the black market); turning non-productive factory buildings into workers' hostels to ease the low-rent housing shortage; and by requisitioning foodstuff in the countryside to load the stands of the working-class market places. The urban workers, more than the miners, needed help from some source. By late 1919 there were about 3,000 unemployed industrial workers in Pécs[15] out of a total urban labor force of 10,476.[16] With the return of the Hungarian Red Army veterans after August 1, 1919, their families received no more remittances from unoccupied territory in trustworthy "blue money."[17] Indeed, money economy had nearly come to an end in the occupied city. Again, the Yugoslav authorities stepped into the breach and restored faith in banknotes by first rubber-stamping them with Cyrillic-lettered guarantees of redemption, and later by affixing to them gum-backed and cancelled official SHS revenue stamps stating their convertibility into Yugoslav *dinars.*[18] Money and price anarchy would have been complete in Pécs without these measures, but the Hungarian Government was worried about its eventual responsibilty for redeeming the stamped bank notes.[18a]

Beginning with August 1919 the basic attitude of the Pécs proletarian Left to the occupiers was determined by a recognition of the fact that their presence prevented the irruption of the White Terror into occupied territory. This was a complete reversal of the climate of opinion during the spring and summer of 1919, when the Right was dreading the intrusion of the Red Terror into occupied Baranya. The news that on August 1, 1919 — the day the Hungarian Soviets fell in Budapest — twenty-two leftist workers were arrested and tortured by the "Whites" in Sásd in unoccupied north Baranya,[19] struck terror in the hearts of the Red Army veterans south of the line of demarcation. There was misery, to be sure, in the occupied south, but at least it was mitigated to some extent by the protective Yugoslavs and, in any event, one could no longer hope for a liberating Red Army to come marching down from the north to establish a workers' paradise in Pécs. News arrived of the wanton murder in Budapest on February 17 of the editor and leading columnist of the Social Democratic daily *Népszava (People's Voice).*[20] Reacting vehemently to the bloody event, a mass meeting of Pécs Socialist workers on February 26 declared itself in favor of continued Yugoslav occupation of Baranya for the duration of the White Terror in unoccupied territory.[21] The report of the French military representative to Paris described the workers' declaration as "veritable treason to their homeland."[22]

The radicalization and leftward shift of the Pécs labor movement was facilitated by another measure of the occupiers. The miners returning from the north were imprudently scattered over a twenty-mile radius in the mining area,[23] thus increasing the possibilities of agitation and of forming new clandestine cells. The Yugoslavs turned over the streets of Pécs to the proletarian masses for ideological and political marches and demonstrations. On March 15 they held a protective umbrella over a mass meeting which endorsed the earlier (February 26, 1920) declaration in favor of a continued Yugoslav occupation and ranged the Pécs labor movement on the side of the Comintern, the new international revolutionary organization set up in Moscow the year before (March 2, 1919). On March 21, 1920 they saw to the maintenance of order while the workers were commemorating the first anniversary of the fallen Hungarian Soviets. On May 1, 1920, for the first time since the beginning of the occupation, the Yugoslav authorities permitted the celebration of International Labor Day. The streetcars stopped running, vehicular traffic disappeared, while a mass of humanity under red flags and slogan-bearing banners swept down from the central Széchenyi Place along the arterial Király (now Kossuth) Street, rhythmically cheering the Communist International; damning and confining to the fires of hell Horthy, the hated "sailor on horseback"; and calling on the proletarians of the world to unite. Thousands of voices sang the revolutionary hymn of the Pécs workers (the International was not yet known):

> The proletarian's sacrifice is blood,
> Blood!
> A coward he who's afraid!
> To battle then, boldly,
> Under the flag,
> Perish all that's bourgeois!

If the ideological content of this May-first demonstration grated on the ears of the proconsuls of Yugoslavia, they should have felt satisfied by the recurring chant:

> Horthy shall not enter here!

Yugoslav permissiveness had a favorable effect on the continuing

increase of SDP and trade union membership.[24] The Christian Socialists joined the Social Democrats *en masse.* The Communists, who
managed to keep in touch with party headquarters in Vienna, Budapest, and Belgrade, were increasingly coming out into the open.[25] The
CPH, illegal in the north since the fall of Béla Kun in August 1919,
began enjoying a tacitly recognized *de facto* existence in Baranya.
Even Dr. Alexander Doktor, the free-thinking President of the Pécs
National Council, became a Communist Party member.[26] A Comin-
tern-oriented Popular Front seemed to be emerging, ideologically
linked to Moscow though politically promoting the regional interests
of conservative Yugoslavia. Annexionist agents from Belgrade and
from Novi Sad in the Bachka were hard at work not only among the
rank-and-file of the labor movement, but also within the inner councils of the Popular Front. Their leader was said to be János Polácsi, an
ex-school teacher from the rural hinterland.[27]

The Pécs Right sullenly watched from behind closed windows the
seeming proletarian dominance of streets and squares. It was, however, confidently looking forward to the day, not too far off, when the
conservative prewar establishment would once again resume its
hereditary rule in a Pécs reunited with what was left of Hungary. News
arriving from the outer world nourished these hopes. It was being
whispered that the peace treaty, a preliminary text of which had been
handed the Hungarian delegation in Paris on January 15, 1920, would
fix the new Yugoslav-Hungarian frontier in a way disappointing to
both the occupiers and their proletarian protégés. In Baranya County
the new border would run south not only of the military line of
demarcation, but also far to the south of the Belgrade Convention
boundary, returning Pécs and most of Baranya, including the coal
mines, to Hungarian sovereignty. Yugoslavia would get only the
southeasternmost tip of the county, in the shape of a triangle formed,
on two sides, by the Danube and Drava rivers, and on its third,
northern face by an international frontier drawn from the village of
Kiskőszeg on the Danube to the hamlet of Bolmány on the Drava, in
the vicinity of Karasica Brook.[28] The presence in Pécs on two occasions of Captain Kálmán Hardy[29] of the Hungarian National Army, a
Pécs native, attached as a liaison officer to the Allied Moore mission,
which first arrived in Pécs on November 30, 1919, was interpreted as
something of a "mandate of heaven" granted to the Horthy régime by
the Great Powers in Paris. It was also considered significant that,
while in Pécs, US Lt. Col. Moore was alleged to have recommended to
the Yugoslav Commanding Officer an augmentation in the size of the

city's Hungarian police force, which by early 1920 had been reduced to 160 men supervised by 60 Yugoslav police officers.[30] Inexplicably, in the midst of the Serb-Left lovefeast, Andor Nendtvich, the conservative old-régime mayor, who had been expelled from and then allowed to return to occupied Baranya in the course of gyrations since 1918, was still in his office in City Hall. Did Nendtvich's presence also point to the shape of things to come? It was said that a shadow Hungarian administration, ready to assume control of the city at a signal, was already in Pécs. Even the names of the new governors were widely known: Count George Pallavicini as Government Commissioner for all of Transdanubia (western Hungary enclosed by the Danube river); Iván Blaskovics as Prefect of both Pécs and Baranya; Julius Gosztonyi (and later Ferenc Keresztes-Fischer) as Government Commissioner for Pécs; and Lt. Col. Alexander Riffl as military commander of Baranya County.[31]

Either the Right had begun showing too much confidence or the Yugoslav occupying administration started losing its cool because at the end of 1919 a crackdown on the local Right began. Starting on December 11, 1919 and culminating in January of the following year, seventeen former Hungarian military officers, among them Lt. Col. Riffl, had their houses searched and were arrested on charges of conspiracy, espionage, and illegal recruitment of armed forces.[32] When the Interallied Military Commission (IMC) was established in Pécs subsequent to these arrests (May 28, 1920), the Right wishfully and correctly interpreted this event, too, as a portent of an impending Yugoslav evacuation.

A week after the arrival of the IMC in Pécs, news was received from Paris, jubilantly by the Right and mournfully by the Left, that the Hungarian peace treaty had been signed and that the victors had awarded most of Baranya, as far south as Karasica Brook, to Hungary. The Right was ready to accept, although the delineation of the new international frontier entailed a minor loss of Hungarian territory. But the Left balked and swore to prevent the entry of Horthy's troops, treaty or no treaty.

Baranya and Peacemaking:
Nationalism and Socialism
Don't Mix in Paris

Except for its sponsorship of the Baranya Reds, Yugoslavia's anti-Communist credentials at the peace conference would have been as impeccable as Czechoslovakia's or Rumania's. At home, in "old Serbia," and in all the new territories gathered under its rule except for Baranya, Belgrade treated its proletarian extreme Left as was then expected of client states in Paris. The Big Four who presided over peacemaking had to maneuver between a right-wing upsurge inside the victor nations and the countervailing pro-Moscow sympathies of Western labor stirred to greater militancy by the Russian Revolution.[1] The Communist threat thus had to be contained with difficulty short of outright Allied intervention, especially after it had been tried in Russia on a small scale, with disastrous results. In this strategic concept the succession states of the Habsburg Monarchy were heavily counted upon. Yugoslavia was expected to be one of the guardians of the *cordon sanitaire*.

Communism of the Russian variety arrived in the lands about to become Yugoslav shortly after the collapse of the Russian front in October 1917. It came with South Slav deserters from the Austro-Hungarian armies returning to their homes in Croatia, the Bachka, Slavonia, and Bosnia. Popular discontent, the lack of food in the countryside, and general misery after three years of war provided a fertile soil for the revolutionary ideas brought by the deserters.[2] The unrest spread to units of the Austro-Hungarian Navy — manned mostly by Croatians and Dalmatians — riding at anchor during the closing months of the war, bottled up in the North Adriatic ports of Pola (Pula) and Cattaro (Kotor). It was during the sailors' mutinies in these ports during February 1918 that Admiral Nicholas Horthy, the last Commander-in-Chief of the Habsburg Fleet, first called attention to himself as a potential counterrevolutionary strong man. The collapse of the Austro-Hungarian Empire and the rise of the Yugoslav Kingdom found well-organized Communist units in all component parts of the new state. These units sought merger with the various Social Democratic Parties which had existed in Serbia, Croatia, Bosnia, Slovenia, and in occupied parts of Hungary since the end of the nineteenth century.[3] By April 1920 those Yugoslav Communists and Social Democrats who had merged were demanding affiliation with the Third or Communist International — the Comintern — formed in Moscow the year before. In June 1920, with the fall of the Hungarian Soviets still a fresh memory, the Yugoslav Communists defiantly proclaimed their Vukovar Program. The goals sought included the creation of a Soviet republic in Yugoslavia, establishment of a Red Army, expropriation and socialization of all manufactures and commerce, requisitioning of housing, and abolition of all debts as well as taxes.[4] This was "left-wing Communism," whose leaders maintained contact with both Russian and Hungarian Communist mentors.

As discussions began at the peace conference, the Yugoslav Government's stance was thus somewhat ambivalent. It seemed to be conservative and anti-Communist at home, but in occupied Baranya it was reportedly favorable to a Bolshevik régime. Could Yugoslavia be counted upon as a determined guardian of the *cordon sanitaire,* the same as Rumania and Czechoslovakia? Was the ambivalence of the Yugoslav negotiating position in Paris simply an unfortunate result of the overzealous comportment of Bachka proconsuls in Baranya, such as Rayitch, who protected and politically utilized the Reds in Pécs not out of ideological convictions but prompted by a Greater Serbia chauvinism? If so, why was the error not corrected even after the Paris visit in the fall of 1919 of Colonel Cholak-Antitch, the skilled Yugoslav military diplomat, who must have been aware of the continental anti-Bolshevik strategy motivating the principal peacemakers? But Belgrade never interfered with the pro-Communist course of its Baranya proconsuls, although there is reason to believe that Cholak-Antitch and his military superiors knew that administrative funds sent by the Belgrade Ministry of Interior to Pécs were being diverted by Rayitch to subsidize the local leftwingers.[5] It was for a lack of funds transferred but apparently not properly disbursed that during the winter of 1920–21 the Central Post Office in Pécs had to close down because it could not be heated,[6] and the hospitals were on the verge of discharging their in-patients for the same reason coupled with a shortage of money to buy food.[7] Why could the Serb falcon not hear the French falconer?

As the peace conference opened, Yugoslav territorial demands against Hungary extended northward to the line of illegal military occupation west of the Danube, from Baja to St. Gotthard on the Austrian frontier.[8] This must have struck the Allied experts, who had their ethnographic maps of the contested area, as an unreasonable demand.[9] The peacemakers were aware of Prince Regent Alexander's instructions, also issued as a proclamation, to the Yugoslav delegation in Paris. The Prince Regent's instructions enjoined on his representatives strict adherence to the principle of nationality and specified that Yugoslavia must "ask only for the ethnographic frontiers of our people."[10] This limitation, of course, could be and probably was interpreted by the delegates as referring to a northern line beyond which no South Slavs lived and not to an ethnic boundary separating Yugoslav and Hungarian majorities. Baranya, however, was not the only area of conflicting Yugoslav-Hungarian territorial demands that had to be discussed in Paris. The county was important because of its coal, a problem open to solution by means other than territorial readjustments. It was probably for this reason, the possibility of a nonterritorial solution for the problem posed by coal, that when discussions at the conference turned to Baranya in early March 1920, the Yugoslav diplomatic line was not nearly as rigid as were the maximalist demands of the Yugoslav administrators in Pécs. Without too much difficulty agreement was reached on a partial line along the course of the Drava to its confluence with the Mura River.[11] This frontier left the major part of Baranya, with Pécs and the coalfields, under Hungarian sovereignty. The relative ease with which the Yugoslav delegation accepted this proposed frontier caused some raised diplomatic eyebrows. The Italians at the conference began circulating reports about an alleged deal between the Yugoslav and Hungarian delegations. It was whispered that, in return for Hungarian support of the Yugoslav claim to the Adriatic port-city of Fiume (Rijeka), the Yugoslav delegation showed itself amenable to making territorial concessions to the Hungarians both in the Bachka and in Baranya.[12]

But this was only idle talk. Actually, by the time the Hungarian peace delegation arrived in Paris (January 7, 1920),[13] the Yugoslav-Hungarian frontier and the future of the Pécs coalfields had been delineated and clarified in two basic documents respectively dated April 6, 1919 and November 7, 1919. The first document had been worked out by the Allied Committee for the Study of Territorial Questions during the final months of the Károlyi régime and was submitted to the Supreme Council on April 6, 1919, less than three weeks after

Béla Kun's coming to power. As far as Baranya — and its neighboring county of Somogy — were concerned, the Committee proposed that the northern frontier of Yugoslavia should follow the course of the Danube to its confluence with the Drava, and then the bed of the latter river to its merging with the Mura, leaving outside Yugoslavia only small South Slav minorities in the two riparian Hungarian counties.[14]

The second document, dated November 7, 1919 (antedating by a week the evacuation of Budapest by the Rumanian Army and the entry of Admiral Horthy's forces into the city), was a communication from the French Foreign Minister to the French diplomatic representative in Belgrade. This document, which was immediately passed to the Yugoslav Government, specified various sectors of the new Yugoslav-Hungarian frontier as "to be considered final," among them a Baranya boundary more advantageous to Yugoslav ethnic claims than the line proposed in April by the Allied Committee for the Study of Territorial Questions. The frontier proposed in November cut the principal arm of the southward-flowing Danube at the village of Kiskőszeg and continued in a southwesterly direction to a point on the Drava about 10 kilometers east of the village of Alsómiholjác, and thence westward along the Drava to its confluence with the Mura. After giving the geographical details of the frontier "to be considered final," the Pichon memorandum also assured Belgrade that this international boundary was not to be regarded as prejudicial to "the exploitation of the Pécs mines" by Yugoslavia.[15]

This was to be the final disposition of the Baranya territory, division with reserved rights of exploitation, that was agreed to by the signatories of the Treaty of Trianon on June 4, 1920. Part II, Article XXVII of the treaty described the new international boundary cutting across Baranya as

the course of the Drau (Drava) downstream; thence south-eastwards to a point to be chosen about 9 kilometres east of Miholjacdolnji, the old administrative boundary between Hungary and Croatia-Slavonia, modified, however, so as to leave the Gyekenyes-Barcs railway, together with the station of Gola, entirely in Hungarian territory; thence in an easterly direction to point 93 about 3 kilometres south-west of Baranyavár, a line to be fixed on the ground passing north of Torjáncz, Löcs and Benge and south of Kassad, Beremend with its railway station and Illocska; thence in a north-easterly direction to a point to be chosen in the course of the Danube about 8 kilometres north of point 169 (Kiskőszeg). . ."[16]

Part VIII, Annex V, Paragraph I resolved the question of the Pécs coal mines by stating that

> Hungary shall also give, as partial reparation, to the Allied and Associated Powers an option for the annual delivery during the five years following the coming into force of the present Treaty of a quantity of steam coal from the Pécs mine. This quantity will be periodically determined by the Reparation Commission, which will dispose of it for the benefit of the Serb-Croat-Slovene State in conditions fixed by the Commission."[17]

Thus, all told, the treaty awarded Yugoslavia only 1,193 square kilometers (23.4%) of the total prewar Baranya area of 5,106 square kilometers, containing 34 villages of the Baranyavár, Siklós, and Mohács districts,[18] but at the same time it gave her access to the yield of the Pécs mines. Neither Hungary nor Yugoslavia had undue reason to complain about this solution. Hungary gave up less territory in this area than anywhere else along its peripheries, retaining both Pécs and the coalfields. Yugoslavia was satisfied both in its ethnic and economic claims.

But, for the time being, this was only on paper. The treaty would not enter into force until after completion of the ratification process, which might yet take months or years. The entry into force would be marked by an exchange of ratifications at the French Ministry of Foreign Affairs. It was only after the deposition of the ratifications that Yugoslavia would be under obligation to withdraw its military forces to the south side of the new international boundary. Would Belgrade comply?

The Yugoslav-controlled leftist press in Pécs opined that the territorial provisions of the Treaty of Trianon need not be considered as final. In its October 13, 1920 number the Pécs Socialist daily *Munkás (Worker)* attributed to a "Yugoslav statesman" the assertion that a separate Baranya Republic could remain an autonomous state under Yugoslav military occupation even after the ratification process of the Treaty of Trianon had been completed.[19] In its October 29 issue the same paper quoted the newly installed Mayor of Pécs, Béla Linder, as disclaiming any connection between the future of Pécs and the ratifications of the Treaty of Trianon. The city, Linder commented, would not be returned to Hungary until its working population petitioned for its reincorporation.[20] There was certainly no basis for this statement in international law. Linder spoke as a politician to maintain unshaken the foundations of his city government. He tried to satisfy both nationalist and socialist sentiments by tacitly admitting the ethnically and culturally Hungarian character of Pécs, while at the same time rejecting, in the name of the local Left, the exercise of Hungarian sovereignty by the Right.

The occupied status of Baranya thus continued unchanged after the signing of the peace treaty on June 4, 1920. Since the Béla Kun interlude, however, the Hungarian question seemed to have acquired more importance in Paris. The Rumanian occupation of Budapest (August–November 1919) was followed by the establishment of a Conference of Allied Diplomatic Representatives and Generals in the Hungarian capital. The Interallied Military Commission (IMC) in Pécs, dominated by the French Major Raoul Dérain, was reporting to the Conference of Ambassadors in Paris through this intermediate body. In addition to Dérain the IMC in Pécs included also the British Major Foster and the Italian Captain Mando, whose appearance at public functions was usually greeted by scattered applause of anti-occupation elements. Mando's popularity was probably prompted by the pro-Italian sympathies of Hungarian nationalists in the then current Italo-Yugoslav border dispute over the disposition of certain Adriatic areas. The most conspicuous and gregarious member of the IMC, however, was Major Dérain, who quickly became a familiar sight, a small man topped by his *képi,* walking his Dachshund Caton in the streets of the city.

Shortly after his arrival in the spring of 1920, Dérain acquired a Hungarian mistress by the name of Aranka Donáth, a tall and lanky *diseuse* of the local open-air orpheum "Pannonia Stage." Miss Donáth's influence on Major Dérain, and the French officer's role in shaping and determining the final solution of the Baranya problem, should not be underestimated. Dérain had probably been strongly anti-Communist, or was certainly familiar with the firmly rightist attitudes of his army superiors, before his arrival in Pécs. His intimacy with the intensely patriotic Aranka, however, made him completely pro-Hungarian and anti-Yugoslav. His reports were appreciated by the Allied Diplomatic Representatives and Generals in Budapest[21] (who had become sympathetic to the Magyar cause) and deprecated by the French Minister in Belgrade[22] (who through osmosis was beginning to share his hosts' antipathy for the Hungarians).

The whole story — the *petite histoire* — of the Dérain-Donáth team was told only after the Yugoslav evacuation of Baranya by the leftist tabloid *Az Ucca (The Street),* a Hungarian-language magazine which saw fit to retreat with the occupiers across the Danube to the annexed town of Novi Sad. If *Az Ucca* is to be believed (French Minister Clément-Simon in Belgrade gave it enough credence to have its pertinent article translated and pouched to Paris),[23] Miss Donáth's political influence on Major Dérain first became apparent when the French officer began wearing his blond mustachios pointing upward *à la hongroise* (though at times he let them droop *à la russe*). According to the tabloid, the Franco-Hungarian couple spent their evenings in Pécs, Raoul listening to Aranka's *viva voce* translations of the local Hungarian press. The *diseuse* thus became in effect a secretary of the IMC,[24] into whose typewriter the Allied observer may have dictated his political reports for Paris. Having become familiar with all IMC secrets, Aranka allegedly proceeded to pass them on to the Hungarian Ministry of Foreign Affairs in Budapest, not without considerable monetary compensation. While this was going on, Dérain lived in the house of Joseph Littke, owner and manager of the local Littke champagne distillery and a pillar of the Right. At champagne dinners given by this capitalist, patriotic Aranka was the toast of the assembled Pécs high society. In brief, through Aranka's influence Dérain became integrated with and assimilated to the nationalist, anti-socialist Right, a formidable underground force in Pécs since the fall of Béla Kun in working for an end of the Yugoslav occupation.

However it may have been, Miss Donáth was believed to be Major Dérain's mistress while the Baranya problem was proceeding slow-motion to its final solution. Dérain's reports from Pécs were approvingly forwarded by the Allied Diplomatic Representatives in Budapest and attentively read by members of the Conference of Ambassadors and other high policymaking bodies in Paris. The reports were outspoken in their criticism of the Yugoslav occupiers and devastating in their hostility to the left-wing régime sponsored by the Yugoslavs. Dérain's "Calendar of Events in Pécs, November 1918–November 1920"[25] and the transcript of his verbal report in Budapest on February 26, 1921 to the Conference of Allied Diplomatic Representatives and Generals,[26] contain a long list of Yugoslav violations, atrocities, depredations, arbitrary requisitionings, and removals. Both documents stress Yugoslav duplicity in establishing and encouraging "a veritable Communist régime" which might soon constitute a threat to the peace of Europe.[27] Allied policymaking was indubitably influenced by Dérain's reporting, from his own passionately focused optic, during the critical period which followed the signing of the Hungarian peace treaty in the spring of 1920 and ended in its application to the Yugoslav-Hungarian frontier during the summer of 1921.

VII

Baranya and the Treaty of Trianon: The Divorce of Nationalism and Socialism

Had the Hungarian peace treaty been signed twelve months earlier, with Béla Kun's "red" régime rather than in mid-1920 with Admiral Horthy's "white" government, the anti-Bolshevik containment policy of the Allies might have shown more accommodation for the territorial demands of the succession states. But by 1920 de-bolshevized Hungary was also a part of the *cordon sanitaire* erected against the Soviets and a new Károlyi fiasco — collapse of a non-Communist régime because of excessive territorial truncation — could not be risked. Consequently, the Rumanians had to be satisfied with less than the Tisza River line as their western frontier; the Czechoslovaks were kept north of the Salgótarján coal mines; and the Yugoslavs were brought to accept a boundary well to the south of the Mecsek massif. The latter apparently signed in a revisionist spirit because, for fifteen months following the signing, they continued their effort to cling to their military frontiers north of the new treaty line. Ideologically analyzed, the Yugoslavs' attempt in 1920–21 to accomplish this objective was to satisfy their own nationalism while promoting their protégés' socialism. In the Middle Europe of 1920–21 this was a diplomatic impossibility.

In the case of the protégés a choice had to be made between the two ideologies. The left-wing socialist régime in Pécs could continue to exist only in detachment from Horthy Hungary. How could detachment be maintained? Theoretically, by jettisoning the Hungarian nationalist aim of Baranya's reunification with Hungary in favor of proletarian internationalism. Strategically, by persevering in the forlorn hope that the armies of Soviet Russia, now successfully ensconced on the Black Sea littoral, would by their mere presence reduce French hegemonial influence in Middle Europe. During the time remaining before the completion of the treaty ratification process, new power relations and yet untried diplomatic maneuvers might work to the advantage of a Left-ruled Baranya. A variant form of the 1919 Károlyi-

Vix syndrome[1] made its appearance in Pécs: abandoned to our enemies by the West, we will be saved by our friends in the East. In Budapest neither public opinion nor the government was in favor of early ratification of a treaty Hungarians considered as a major national disaster, transcending the Baranya question by far. In fact, Foreign Minister Count Teleki instructed the diplomatic representative of the Hungarian Government in Paris on June 18, 1920 that "the ratification of the peace treaty must be delayed as long as possible."[2] On June 24 the referent of Hungarian affairs at the Quai d'Orsay reassured the Hungarians that, although "the French Government was willing to bring about the early evacuation of Pécs, Baranya and other territories," such areas would be evacuated by the Yugoslavs probably "only three months after the ratification of the peace treaty."[3]

The eastward Baranya drift began a week after the signing of the Treaty of Trianon. On June 12 the Pécs Social Democratic Party officially changed its name to "Socialist Party in Pécs" (SPP).[4] This was done to symbolize the new orientation toward the Third or Communist International (Comintern). Events outside the Baranya microcosm seemed to justify the hope that cooperation with the Comintern was the correct course for the Baranya Left in the circumstances. On July 27, 1920 the Russian Red Army invaded Poland and by August 14 stood at the gates of Warsaw. On August 9 the British Labor Party and its affiliated trade unions began making preparations for a general strike should the United Kingdom declare war on the Soviets. During the Soviet advance in Pécs the leftist press proclaimed victory for the international proletariat and washed its hands of nationalism.[5] "Our enemies," wrote the Pécs *Munkás (Worker)*, "are the Social Democrats, the social patriots, and the social chauvinists."[6] Although the French saved Warsaw and the Russians had to retreat east beyond a border advantageous to Poland, the Civil War in their own country was going well for the Soviets. In November 1920 it ended in a complete Reds-over-Whites victory. In anticipation of this event, the Socialist Party in Pécs (SPP) formally declared its adherence to the Comintern in October 1920.[7] At the Third Congress of the Comintern, which opened in Moscow on July 22, 1921, the SPP was represented by two invited delegates from Pécs, the chemical industry worker Rudolph Wommert and the miner Richard Friedl. The two SPP representatives, who had deliberating but not voting rights, submitted a lengthy and detailed report on the Pécs-Baranya situation to the Congress (see Appendix 2-B).[7a]

The new affiliation did not disqualify the Pécs Socialists from Yugoslav backing. In rapid succession, first, the defunct (since 1919) Pécs National Council was reestablished at Socialist demand; next, the Council ordered elections for a new municipal governing body of 100 members. The elections took place under Yugoslav supervision on August 29–30, before the public announcement of the Comintern ties, and resulted in an overwhelming Socialist victory.[8] The franchise and the balloting were reportedly less democratic than in a British or French election.[9] The protesting conservative Mayor Andor Nendtvich, who through some oversight was still sitting behind his desk in his City Hall office, was summarily arrested and deported into unoccupied Hungary.[10] He was replaced by Béla Linder,[11] Minister of War in the fallen Károlyi régime, sole Hungarian signer of the Belgrade Military Convention, who had made himself famous for the Left, and infamous for the Right, by his 1918 declaration: "I don't want to see soldiers anymore!" Under Béla Kun, Linder was entrusted with diplomatic missions abroad. Major Dérain, who closely observed Linder's arrival and work in Pécs, described the newcomer as an idealist and an honest man, but just an instrument of the Socialist Party.[12] British Minister Young in Belgrade, who later received Linder at the request of the Yugoslav Foreign Office, said he was a "very elegant man," with prematurely gray hair, hard to place politically.[13] Both Dérain and Young agreed that Linder's immediate objective was a prolongation of the Yugoslav occupation in an autonomous Baranya, for possibly five years, at the end of which a plebiscite should decide the final disposition of the territory. Young added, apprehensively, that since Linder was put in his Pécs office by the Yugoslavs and subsequently became a regular visitor to Belgrade, one could not completely reject the hypothesis that Belgrade had worked out a "Machiavellian plan" for the time it would no longer have an excuse to stay in non-treaty Hungarian territory.[14]

The experts of the Conference of Ambassadors in Paris correctly analyzed Yugoslav motivation and intentions vis-à-vis Baranya as primarily centered on coal. For the most part the railroads of Yugoslavia were propelled by Pécs coal. "It is for this reason that the SHS state has prolonged, *contre tout droit,* the occupation of this region."[15] To solve the vexing problem of coal, the experts recommended that attention should continue to be focused on the pertinent provisions (Paragraph One, Part VIII, Annex V) of the Treaty of Trianon.[16] Under this section of the peace treaty Yugoslavia was entitled, as partial reparations from Hungary, to an option on annual deliveries for five years from the Pécs mines of a certain quantity of steam coal *(charbon de traction)*, to be fixed periodically by the Reparations Commission.[17] Until Belgrade had a firm commitment from the Reparations Commission, the experts' argument ran, it would continue to refuse to evacuate.[18] Accordingly, in order to remove all obstacles to a future evacuation, on December 15, 1920 the Conference of Ambassadors invited the Reparations Commission to take measures that the pertinent provisions of the Treaty of Trianon regarding the exploitation of the Pécs coal mines were applied, implemented, and carried out under its control.[19] It was not until May 7, 1921, however, that the Conference of Ambassadors was able to convey to the Hungarian Government the decision of the Reparations Commission regarding the implementation of the pertinent provisions of the Treaty of Trianon regarding the Pécs mines. The Commission had decided, the Hungarians were told, that the Yugoslavs were to be entitled "for the first year, to receive 54% of the net production of the mines in the Pécs basin . . . [and that] this percentage shall be maintained after the first year unless another figure should be adopted."[20] Bilateral negotiations between Hungary and Yugoslavia (which wanted 60%) on the question of Pécs coal continued unabated in Belgrade nearly until the end of the occupation.[21]

The work of quiet diplomacy was thus not to bear fruit for many months. In the meantime the clash of pro- and counter-evacuation forces continued both nationally and internationally. On December 12, 1920, three days before the Conference of Ambassadors decided to tie up evacuation and coal in one package, there was another mass meeting of workers and citizens in Széchenyi Place in Pécs. The assembly noted with satisfaction that most of occupied Baranya was to be returned to Hungary according to the provisions of the peace treaty. Then, neatly separating nationalism from socialism, an appeal was made to the occupying Yugoslav power to prolong its presence in county and city, so as to provide Horthy Hungary with the example of a real democratic state on its borders.[22]

The coal-for-evacuation formula of the Paris experts would prove to be the correct compromise solution for the Baranya problem, but the diplomatic process continued to work very slowly. At the end of February 1921 there was still no reply either from the Reparations Commission or from the Yugoslav Government to the communications addressed to them, respectively, on December 15 and 20 by the Conference of Ambassadors. Indeed, it developed that the Yugoslav Government had not yet been informed; only the Allied diplomatic representatives in Belgrade had received word. The British Embassy in

Paris therefore opined in a memorandum dated February 22, 1921 that "it would be advisable to ascertain, before officially informing Belgrade, whether the Reparations Commission was in agreement" with the Ambassadors' December 15, 1920 coal-and-evacuation formula.[23] On February 24 the Embassy's proposal was adopted by the Ambassadors and a resolution was voted by the Conference to invite the Reparations Commission to answer the Ambassadors' communication of December 27, 1920 relative to the Pécs mines.[24] A month later, still waiting for a reply from the Commission to the Conference, the French Government made a languid attempt to probe into Yugoslav policy toward occupied Hungarian territory. The essay brought no concrete results except establishing that Belgrade was apparently more intransigent than Paris had presumed it to be.

The occasion was French Vice Admiral Fatou's special mission to Belgrade on March 20-30, 1921 to discuss Yugoslav participation in the projected Porto Rosa conference on communications. Admiral Fatou, who during the war was in command of French naval units which protected Serbian troop convoys to the Salonika front from the island of Corfu, was received on March 22 by Yugoslav Premier Pashitch as *persona grata* but was handed over for meaningful conversations to Secretary General of the Foreign Office Popovitch. The latter displayed a "slightly defiant attitude"[25] toward his distinguished French guest and, on March 24, somewhat prophetically raised the danger of a Habsburg restoration threatening in Hungary.[26] Two days later, on March 26, ex-King-Emperor Charles of erstwhile Austria-Hungary landed by airplane in the west-Hungarian town of Szombathely in an abortive *putsch*-like attempt to regain his throne, if not in Vienna, at least in Budapest. A Habsburg restoration, which could be a first step toward the resurgence of the Dual Monarchy dismembered in favor of the succession states, might be a suitable excuse for Yugoslav troops to remain in occupation of Hungarian soil in temporary disregard of treaty provisions. The Habsburg danger seemed real at the time not only to the directly-concerned Little Entente (Czechoslovakia, Rumania, and Yugoslavia) but also the more distantly-affected Great Powers. The Yugoslavs took the Habsburg threat so seriously that, immediately after Charles's ill-fated landing at Szombathely, the Yugoslav representative in Budapest called on Regent Horthy himself and declared in the name of his government that the attempted *putsch* "was a *casus belli* for Yugoslavia . . . Yugoslavia [being] primarily responsible for the decision of the Allied Powers against the restoration of the Habsburgs."[27]

Popovitch played on the common political idiosyncrasy. The Hungarians, he told Fatou, actually have an army of 200,000 at their disposal instead of the 35,000 permitted them by the Treaty of Trianon. Such a military force could threaten the peace of Middle Europe. The Yugoslavs, he claimed, were better judges of the regional situation than anybody; they could see far more clearly than the French and the British, who had made mistakes before in the Balkans. As for Baranya? It was only a function of a larger complex of problems. Fatou, content with getting a promise of Yugoslav presence at Porto Rosa, shrugged it off while putting on the record Belgrade's intransigence with a fatuously paraphrased remark borrowed from Voltaire: "Everything was for the best in the best of Yugoslavias"[28] — for the Yugoslav Government.

During the diplomatic standstill rumors with and without foundation were circulating — or were being circulated — in occupied Baranya. The Yugoslavs, it was said, would not be leaving until the Hungarians evacuated and, in accordance with the Treaty of Trianon, turned over to Austria the present Burgenland, then known as Western Hungary (to the Hungarians) and, in part, as "Austro-Serb territories" (to the Yugoslavs.[29] It was remembered that the Yugoslavs also occupied other non-treaty Hungarian territories, including the strategic Szeged city suburb of Ujszeged on the left bank of the Tisza River.[30] A Baranya evacuation, it was intimated, might result in prolonged Ujszeged occupation. Also, the Hungarians would have to carry out the disarmament clauses of the treaty before any of their occupied, non-treaty territories could be returned to them.[31] Another, logically if not pragmatically convincing argument for continued Yugoslav occupation seemed to be the obvious analogy, because of coal, between Baranya and the Saarland, an area given special status in the Treaty of Versailles. Rumors spread, or were spread, that, under a new international agreement already being negotiated, Baranya and the Pécs coalfields would be placed under League of Nations control for a period of fifteen years, during which the Yugoslav military occupation would continue and the yield of the mines would be reserved for Yugoslavia. At the end of fifteen years, a plebiscite would determine under what sovereignty the territory should be placed.[32]

Everybody knew that something was in the air. On July 31, 1920 the Hungarian Foreign Ministry warned Paris that the "Social Democrats in Pécs are planning a *coup d'état* at the beginning of August with the assistance of Yugoslav authorities" and threatened to resort to armed intervention should the *coup* take place.[33] Béla Linder's frequent absences from his mayoral office appeared to substantiate such reports. Linder became a diplomat at large for his Yugoslav-protected Pécs régime. It was no secret that he was trying to negotiate with the occupying power autonomous status for Baranya and to gain the assent of the Little Entente as well as the Great Powers for such a diplomatic *modus vivendi.* Before leaving for Belgrade in November 1920 he did inform the Interallied Military Commission in Pécs that the agenda of his visit to the Yugoslav capital included seeking autonomy for Baranya.[34] Early in January he met with Yugoslav Interior Minister Drashkovitch in occupied Baja on the Danube, again to discuss Baranya self-rule. Later in the month Young reported from Belgrade that Oscar Jászi, the leading intellect of the exiled Károlyi government, was supporting Linder in the establishment of an autonomous Baranya, eventually to serve as a jumping-off place for a struggle against the Horthy régime.[35] On March 2, 1921 Linder addressed identical notes, lengthy anti-Horthy and anti-Habsburg diatribes, to the Foreign Ministers of Czechoslovakia, Rumania, and Yugoslavia, pleading for continued Yugoslav occupation of Baranya until Hungary was once more under a democratic form of government.[36] Linder continued this para-diplomatic activity probably in ignorance of the fact that on April 27 and May 3, 1921 the Yugoslav Government received two decisive diplomatic communications from the Conference of Ambassadors in Paris. The first of these two communications informed Belgrade that, upon completion of the treaty ratification process, it would be expected to evacuate non-treaty Hungarian territory.[37] The second communication invited the Yugoslavs to start preparations for a Baranya evacuation.[38]

During May 1921, in the course of one of Linder's visits to Belgrade, the Yugoslav Foreign Ministry set up meetings for the Pécs Mayor with the French and British Ministers. Both diplomats submitted reports of their conversations, which were in the hands of the Conference of Ambassadors by early June. The British Minister reported that on May 16 he had listened impassively to the following presentation by Linder:

The Pécs-Baranya area has a population of about 300,000 souls. The inhabitants are politically advanced and should not be reincorporated into reactionary Hungary until a democratic government is re-established in that country. Reunion with Hungary at this time would bring reprisals in Baranya. Without a prolongation of the Yugoslav occupation, without the establishment of an autonomous Baranya régime to radiate democracy into Horthy Hungary, the local proletariat would be forced to destroy the mines — in which British capital is invested. There would be violent resistance to the entry of Horthy's troops and the workers would probably demolish the factories before they fled the area. To avoid all this, Baranya should be internationalized as a part of the "Danube régime" — placed under the International Commission for the Danube — with Yugoslav occupation prolonged for maximum five years, minimum one year, as a guarantee that Hungary complies with all the provisions of the peace treaty. Pécs is not a Bolshevik enclave in any sense; private property rights are respected.[39] A document containing these statements and proposals was left with Young, as well as with the French, Italian, and Little Entente diplomatic representatives in the Yugoslav capital.

Was Linder a sincere protagonist of the rights of peoples or simply an instrument of the Yugoslav Government employed to retain control of the Pécs mines? — asked Young in his report and immediately confessed that he could not answer his own question.[40] His superiors in London and Paris took no interest in Linder's political personality; they were concerned only with the overall diplomatic problem: the continued improper military occupation of territory belonging to another sovereignty. Conservative public opinion in the West was getting stirred up. There were interpellations in the House of Lords on March 7, 17, and May 5.[41] Lord Curzon, Foreign Secretary, told the Lords on May 5 that "every measure will be put upon them [the Yugoslavs] by His Majesty's Government to terminate the occupation" of non-treaty Baranya.[42] This was not an idle figure of speech. In submitting Young's Belgrade memorandum of conversation to the Conference of Ambassadors, the British Embassy in Paris suggested to that body in mid-June that (1) the Interallied Military Commission in Pécs supervise and impose an evacuation of all Yugoslav-occupied [non-treaty] Hungarian territory; and that (2) the Allied diplomatic representatives in Belgrade inform the SHS Government of the foregoing, simultaneously requesting an immediate reply to the May 3, 1921 note of the Conference of Ambassadors to the Yugoslav Legation in Paris.[43] In this communication, still unanswered, Belgrade had been invited to declare its intention to evacuate the contested Hungarian areas as soon as the Treaty of Trianon entered into force.

The Conference of Ambassadors was quite familiar with the diplomatic as well as strategic aspects of the Baranya question in its relationship to the overall policy of Soviet containment. The deliberations of the Conference showed concern not only with a military occupation unjustified by international law but also with the possibility that the

occupied area could, under a militantly leftist régime, present an
advance base for east-to-west Soviet military movements. The latter
assumption was based to a large degree on transmittals of Major
Dérain's weekly reports from Pécs. These missives left little doubt in
policymaking Allied minds about the ideological affinities and strategic potentialities of the Yugoslav-supported and Comintern-affiliated régime in Baranya. As early as October 31, 1920 Dérain had
reported that the new Pécs Municipal Council just established was "an
oppressive régime not mitigated by the Yugoslav authorities."[44] In
subsequent weekly reports the French Major claimed that the moving
spirit of the Pécs Municipal Council, the Socialist Party in Pécs,
"represented by Linder, created and protected by Rayitch, was openly
and violently Communist";[45] and that a Communist organization was
being completed in Pécs possibly for a Soviet Russian offensive in the
spring of 1921.[46] The likelihood of such a military operation made it
urgent, Dérain recommended, "to smash without delay this Communist régime."[47] Warning of such gravity from a trained military
observer, supported by Fouchet, the French High Commissioner in
Budapest, could not be taken lightly by Allied policymakers on the
morrow of the Soviet victory in the Russian Civil War (November
1920), especially in the light of the militantly pro-Soviet sympathies
being then demonstrated by British and French labor. In December
1920 the French Chargé d'Affaires in Budapest reported to his government that "the existence of a nest of armed Bolsheviks in Pécs would
be [in the event of a Soviet westward offensive] a terrible danger for
the civilized world."[48] In February 1921 the Conference of Allied
Diplomatic Representatives sitting in Budapest invited Dérain to
come up from Pécs and to give a general verbal report on the situation
in occupied Baranya. A transcript of Dérain's report and interrogation
was prepared and submitted to the Conference of Ambassadors.

In this lengthy document[49] Dérain identified the gist of the Baranya
problem as the fact that, contrary to the pertinent provisions of The
Hague Regulations and of the Belgrade Military Convention, the
occupying Yugoslav power, having expelled most Hungarian civil
servants from the local government, installed civilian administrators
of its own nationality. These foreign administrators, illegally employed, proceeded "to abuse power, deny justice, arbitrarily requisi-
tion property, unjustifiably levy taxes, establish an impermissible
electoral system, support Communists in power, allow schools to be
set up for Bolshevik propaganda, foment disorder in the area, and
endanger the social order of Middle Europe."[50] After making this

indictment, Dérain recommended that either the Yugoslavs be invited to undertake an immediate evacuation or, short of such a military measure, they should be prevailed upon to "revert to a regular occupation of a purely military character" by removing their irregular, communist-sponsoring civilian administrators. A complete military evacuation, however, would be more in conformity, he thought, with *"l'état actuel de l'Europe"* and with the spirit of the peace treaties.[51]

The Dérain report was submitted to Paris and, pursuant to the recommendation of the Allied Diplomatic Representatives in Budapest, the Baranya problem was again brought before the Conference of Ambassadors. Dérain's recommendations had strong support from his superiors but the Major seemed to have incurred the personal animosity of Clément-Simon, the French Minister in Belgrade, who considered him indelicate and too pro-Hungarian.[52] However, the British officer on the Pécs IMC, a Major Foster, was also of Dérain's opinion. Early in May this British military observer recommended to the Allied Diplomatic Representatives in Budapest that, in order to prevent violence in Baranya, the evacuating Yugoslav Army should start, a month before its withdrawal, replacing Yugoslav administrators with Hungarian civil servants.[53]

In the meantime, in spite of the diplomatic urgings, there was still no reply from Belgrade to the May 3, 1921 note of the Conference of Ambassadors regarding a Yugoslav evacuation of non-treaty Hungarian territories. Showing understandable annoyance, the Ambassadors now had the French Ministry of Foreign Affairs telegraphically instruct its representative in Belgrade to deliver a *démarche* to the Yugoslav Foreign Office, stressing the urgency of a reply to the May 3 note.[54] A paragraph of the telegram instructed Clément-Simon to "repeat" to Premier Pashitch that the latter "should not expect any support from the Government of the French Republic were his government to adopt an attitude which would constitute a formal violation of the treaty."[55] Similar instructions, except of course for the special paragraph for the French Minister, were telegraphed to the British and Italian Ministers in Belgrade. But June passed and nothing happened. An Italian ministerial crisis interfered, making concerted Allied action in Belgrade impossible. Finally, on July 5, 1921, the French Ministry of Foreign Affairs transmitted new instructions to Belgrade from the Conference of Ambassadors. These instructions told the French and British Ministers that they alone, without waiting for their Italian colleague and without further delay, should deliver the *démarche* to the Yugoslav Foreign Office regarding the declaration the Government of Yugoslavia had been asked to make two months earlier on the subject of its intentions concerning a Baranya evacuation.[56]

The *démarche* was made; July passed; but still there was no movement. Only the treaty ratification process progressed silently and invisibly. Finally, on July 26, 1921 the text of the Treaty of Trianon, bearing its last required ratification, was deposited at the Quai d'Orsay.[57] The treaty was now in force. The Yugoslav Army no longer had the right to remain north of the new international frontier. But if it evacuated, the ruling Left in occupied Baranya would dissolve like an insubstantial pageant and leave not a wrack behind. What was the Left to do?

VIII

The Baranya Republic:
Last Stand of the Left

News of the completed treaty ratification process reached Pécs while the Baranya Left was trying to adjust to new Middle European political realities. Since late 1920 protecting Yugoslavia had gradually been turning anti-Communist at home. During the November parliamentary elections of that year there were indications that the Belgrade government was not favorably inclined toward giving the proletarian Left a share in legislative power. Communist candidates began lodging protests that the authorities were using various kinds of pressures to discourage voters from casting ballots for candidates of the extreme Left.[1] Fifty-eight Communist deputies were nevertheless elected out of a total of 419 *skupshtina* members.[2] Following the elections, the Government promulgated a decree for the maintenance of law and order, the so-called *Obznana,* which was principally directed against the Communists.[3] On June 28, 1921 a bombing attempt was made by a Communist on the life of Prince Regent Alexander.[4] On July 21 former Minister of Interior Drashkovitch, who had *ex officio* signed the *Obznana,* and then resigned, was assassinated[5] by a member of a terrorist group called "Red Justice." A mass trial of Communists followed. On August 1, reacting to the flareup of terrorism, the *skupshtina* enacted a "Law Concerning the Protection of Public Security and Order in the State."[6] The new statute was used to expel the fifty-eight Communist deputies from the national legislature and to declare the Communist Party illegal in Yugoslavia.[7]

Thus, by the summer of 1921, the Left in Baranya was wedged in between a counterrevolutionary "white" régime in Hungary to the north and an increasingly anti-Communist Yugoslav kingdom to the south. The common denominator between the two political systems was anti-Communist nationalism. Both wanted Baranya and both were now offering a variety of pacifiers and sweeteners to diminish the number of their opponents in the area. In Hungary the Teleki government had begun the liquidation of the White Terror by ordering the arrest of the sadistic officers grouped in a detachment headquartered in Budapest's Hotel Britannia (November 10, 1920).[8] The completion of the treaty ratification process was agitating the Hungarian National Assembly, whose members kept the matter of the delayed evacuation on the parliamentary agenda by frequent interpellations through the spring and summer of 1921.[9] Replying to one such interpellation, Foreign Minister Dr. Gustav Gratz promised complete amnesty and no reprisals for acts committed in Baranya during the Yugoslav occupation.[10] The Yugoslavs, in their turn, in order to counteract the adverse reaction among their Baranya protégés of their anti-Communist measures at home, began appealing to the landless peasants of the occupied county with promises of land distribution in the event of annexation to Yugoslavia.[11]

The Baranya Left was not easily swayed either by the Hungarian offer of amnesty or by the Yugoslav promise of land reform. The leaders of the Pécs proletariat were faced with the difficult choice between two "law and order" régimes. "White" Hungary had not so far failed to take bloody reprisals against the revolutionary Left fallen from power. As for regressive Yugoslavia, her new anti-Communist laws would certainly be extended to an annexed Baranya, very likely even in the event of just a prolonged protectorate. During mid-1921 AVALA, the official Yugoslav telegraph agency, was reported to have forecast the coming "dissolution of Communist organization" in Pécs by the occupying authorities.[12] Which dismal prospect was the lesser of two evils?

The Left began to split apart on the horns of this dilemma. The completed treaty ratification process had an additional shattering effect because it introduced an element of urgency. Three principal leftist factions emerged. A moderate right wing arose, under the leadership of the attorney Julius Hajdu (who had already played a moderating role at the time of the Sixth Regiment's mutiny in 1918), speaking through the daily *Munkás (Worker)*. This faction considered the Yugoslav occupation as a necessary evil to be endured while the Horthy régime remained in power to the north. An extreme left wing, led by János Polácsi and having the *Pécsi Ujság (Pécs News)* as its press organ, engaged in propaganda for annexation to Yugoslavia at the "spontaneous" request of the Baranya population. In between the two extremes stood the City Hall group of Béla Linder, which was pushing for an autonomous Baranya under the aegis of the League of Nations, protected against external enemies by the Yugoslav Army as a League surrogate.[13]

As early as mid-1920 *Politika,* the semi-official organ of the Yugoslav Government, had reported that a republic, under the protection of the League, was the goal of a "powerful movement" in Baranya.[14] *Proletár,* the mouthpiece of the Hungarian Communist Party then appearing in Vienna, published an editorial entitled "The Baranya Republic" in its December 30, 1920 number. The editorialist saw the issues clearly centered on the necessity of Pécs coal for Yugoslavia. He approved the proposed republic unenthusiastically, describing it as an "émigré illusion," at best a *pis-aller* in the given circumstances. Concluding his analysis the writer warned that "one must look at the Baranya question not merely in a Pécs optique but also in its relation to both Yugoslavia and Hungary, after a full examination of the factors at hand in Middle Europe and in the Balkans."[14a]

The factional struggle over the future of Baranya continued within the Pécs Left. The Polácsist *Pécsi Ujság* accused the Hajdu faction of clandestinely practicing capitalism, but *Munkás* struck back and charged its antagonists with engaging in white slavery.[15] By the end of 1920 the Socialist Party in Pécs lost both its left and right extremes. On November 21 Polácsi was expelled from the party. On December 24 the Yugoslav authorities deported Hajdu from all their territories. The party began falling apart. Its local organizations, notably in Mohács, Siklós, and Baja, seceded from the Pécs center and, by February 1921, were on their own, in direct relationship with Belgrade.

These internal developments reduced the politically effective Baranya Left to its Linder faction, which sought to strengthen itself by an alliance with the Smallholders Party, representative of the land-hungry but anti-Communist peasants. In an attempt to gain the approval of the Great Powers and the Little Entente, as well as to ward off in advance the possibility of falling victim to Belgrade's incipient anti-Communist measures, the Linder group started stressing its lack of Communist ideology and affinity.[16] As proof of their contention, the Linderites pointed to the respect for private property and existence of a multi-party press in Pécs under their rule. They also thought to have solved the foreign political dilemma of whither Baranya. They cast in their lot with Yugoslavia, whose anti-Left repressive measures were yet to be demonstrated locally, rather than with a Hungary under Horthy, whose reprisals against the radical Left were already a matter of the record in unoccupied Baranya. As for the modality of future coexistence with Yugoslavia, it was to be neither Hajdu's simple, apolitical military occupation nor Polácsi's outright annexation, but the already approved formula of a Baranya Republic protected through the Yugoslav Army by the League of Nations.[17] Rayitch, the Yugoslav Prefect in Pécs, pledged his personal support to this proposed solution of the problem,[18] no doubt because it met with his minimum requirements: an indefinite prolongation of Yugoslav control over most of Baranya.

Action leading to the rise and fall of the Baranya Republic took place on three fronts during the three-week period ending on August 19, 1921: in Pécs itself by the Rayitch-manipulated Left; in Belgrade, manifested by Linder's quasi-diplomatic efforts; and in Paris, through regular diplomatic channels between Yugoslavia and the Conference of Ambassadors.

During these three critical weeks the leftist press in Pécs clearly misrepresented Allied intentions by informing its readers that the Allied Supreme Council did not consider a Baranya evacuation timely;[19] that a military intervention by the Little Entente against Hungary was imminent;[20] and that a Yugoslav ultimatum had been delivered in Budapest.[21] Encouraged by such news, the workers of Pécs staged a one-day protest strike on August 12 against evacuation. In a communiqué, also misleading, issued on the following day, Prefect Rayitch stated that "reports of an impending evacuation are without reliable foundations."[22]

It was in this confident spirit that a scheduled trade union conference assembled in Pécs on August 14 to discuss the rising cost of living and to register its disapproval of an evacuation. According to local leftist sources, 15,000 workers and citizens were present in the city's central Széchenyi Place[23] (according to the Allied observers: "4,000 Communists")[24] listening to speeches calling for resistance to Horthy and threatening with destruction of the mines, the factories, and the city itself should the Admiral's troops enter it. At least one of the speakers declared that the intent of the mass meeting was "not to set up a dictatorship of the proletariat or to establish communism but merely to maintain an honest democracy."[25] At this point the painter Péter Dobrovits mounted the rostrum unexpectedly. Dobrovits was a Hungarian citizen of Serbian descent who had spent some time in prison for alleged complicity in the mutiny of the Sixth Regiment in the spring of 1918, but was set free after the October (Károlyi) revolution of that year. Now he faced the crowd in the square and told them:

> . . . the moment has come to declare to the world that we want to be master of our fate and to proclaim the Hungarian-Serbian Baranya Republic. We will at once inform the Belgrade Government of our

decision and will request its approving agreement. Starting with this moment, the fate of Baranya is in the hands of the Executive Committee of the Hungarian-Serbian Baranya Republic. . . Long live the Hungarian-Serbian Baranya Republic![26]

Thunderous approval and a reportedly unanimous show of hands greeted Dobrovits's proclamation. The text of an oath was then read and repeated by the people in the square. Next Dobrovits was chosen by acclamation as President of the new Republic's Executive Committee. Twenty-one members were appointed to this governing body. As the meeting was breaking up, a delegation led by Dobrovits walked down the sloping square to the City Hall at its southern edge to inform Prefect Rayitch of what had taken place. The latter noted the information conveyed to him, promised to inform his government at once by courier and, pending instructions from Belgrade, pledged to "support the workers and Dobrovits."[27] By nightfall posters in Hungarian, Serbo-Croatian, and German covered the walls of the occupied city, informing the inhabitants that, in accordance with the people's right to self-determination, the Serbian-Hungarian Baranya Republic had been proclaimed, that the Republic would divide the land among the working peasants, and that it would place itself under the protection of Yugoslavia and the Little Entente.[28] At a second mass meeting held that evening in front of City Hall, guest speaker Voyin Brkits, a Social Democratic member of the Belgrade *skupshtina,* inveighed against the Bolsheviks and their policies, warning the workers of Pécs not to follow the Russian party line.[29] On August 15 the communes of Mohács, Szigetvár, Siklós, Barcs, and Baja declared their adherence to the Baranya Republic. The following day, Dobrovits left for Belgrade at the head of a delegation, formally to place the new mini-state under Yugoslav protection and to obtain permission for the recruitment of a republican army.[30]

The Baranya Republic was proclaimed in Béla Linder's absence. Between August 3 and 19 the Mayor was engaged in shuttle diplomacy between Pécs and the Yugoslav capital. Although the Yugoslav Government did not seem to be overly optimistic about the future of the Baranya Republic, Linder's reports to his constituents, back home were cheerfully confident. He did pass on Premier Pashitch's ominous assurance that, in the event of an evacuation, Yugoslavia would provide asylum for all political refugees from Baranya,[31] but added that "government circles in Belgrade . . . do not consider timely an evacuation of the occupied territories."[32] Both Linder and Rayitch saw fit to keep secret the information Linder received in Belgrade on August 9 that there was no way to avoid an evacuation.[33]

Indeed, following the events of August 14, the Pécs left-wing press attributed to Linder the statement that "Belgrade government circles have favorably reacted to the proclamation of the Baranya Republic."[34] The press also reported an alleged statement by Pashitch to Linder to the effect that "there is no question now of a Baranya evacuation and there will be none possibly for months yet."[35] On August 18 Linder telephoned from Belgrade to say that not only had Pashitch assured him that a Baranya evacuation was not on the agenda, but also that the Yugoslav Premier "had agreed to equip and arm republican battalions."[36] On August 19 — the day before the Yugoslavs started leaving Pécs — Linder briefly returned to the city and from the balcony of City Hall told a crowd that, although he had brought no orders with him which would assure the maintenance of the occupation, he could state that such orders would not be long delayed.[37]

Until the opening in 1972 of the French Foreign Ministry's archives for the years 1918–1929 there could be a reasonable doubt of the good faith of the Yugoslav Government in not telling Linder and in not instructing Rayitch till the very end that evacuation was only a few days off, that it had been scheduled to start on August 18, and was to be completed on August 24.[37a] The French diplomatic sources now available reveal that up to August 15 the Yugoslav Government had not come to a firm determination to withdraw its troops to the new Trianon frontier and that, indeed, between August 16 and 18 it mounted a last-minute diplomatic offensive to prolong the presence of its armed forces in Baranya. Secret diplomacy succeeded only in postponing the entry of Hungarian troops into the occupied parts by two days (August 18 to August 20) but failed in its larger aspect to prolong the occupation indefinitely, so to save the Baranya Republic.

The Interallied Military Commission (IMC) in Pécs had been designated to oversee the withdrawal of Yugoslav forces from occupied Baranya. When British Colonel Gosset arrived in Pécs on August 11 to take up his post as Chairman of the IMC, it was assumed both in Paris and in Budapest that the evacuation would start on August 18. However, the Yugoslav Government had still not replied to the Allied démarche of June 25. There were other disturbing developments. Belgrade had also ignored an invitation from Paris to appoint a sole military commander for the entire Yugoslav-occupied Hungarian area[38] for a simplified and easily workable liaison with the IMC in Pécs under Colonel Gosset. A new diplomatic roadblock was thrown up on August 16 by Miloyevitch, the Yugoslav diplomatic agent in Budapest, who informed the Allied Diplomatic Representatives in the Hungarian capital that his government "feared complications" should Hungarian troops enter occupied Baranya and that consequently Yugoslav evacuation should be postponed until a later date.[39] Miloyevitch also asked for guarantees for his country, including continued use for coal shipments of the main railroad line from Pécs to the Yugoslav frontier *via* the town of Villány.[40] Then came, on August 18 — instead of a Yugoslav reply to the Allied *démarche* — a note from the Yugoslav Legation in Paris to the Conference of Ambassadors, requesting that the evacuation of Baranya be delayed *(retardée)* "in view of the events now taking place there."[41] This was an obvious reference to the proclamation of the Baranya Republic on August 14 and a Yugoslav diplomatic followup to Linder's entreaties as well as to Dobrovits's request of August 16 for a Yugoslav protectorate.

The Allied supervisory apparatus was thrown into disarray by these Yugoslav diplomatic moves. In Budapest the Allied Diplomatic Representatives handed Miloyevitch "an energetic note" rejecting his request for a delay in evacuation beyond August 18 and dismissing his demand for guarantees.[42] The note added, apprehensively, that owing to Yugoslav dilatoriness in Baranya, Hungarian evacuation of the Burgenland, awarded to Austria by the Treaty of Trianon, had to be postponed from August 21 to August 23.[43] The Conference of Ambassadors was even more stern. In a note dated August 19 and addressed to the Yugoslav Legation in Paris, the previous Allied diplomatic *démarche* to Yugoslavia over Baranya was repeated "in the most pressing manner" and a warning note was added: in the event of Yugoslav non-compliance with the *démarche,* the Conference of Ambassadors envisaged "the most serious complications."[44] As diplomatic language goes, this was mincing no words.

Still the Yugoslavs were not completely subdued, in fact they were heartened, because the evacuation target date of August 18 had passed and their troops were still in Baranya. The Baranya Republic was getting a reprieve, although it would prove to be only of two days. But the rank-and-file of the Pécs Left was still unaware how closely the end had approached. The Yugoslav military knew. On the evening of August 18 Colonel Gosset in Pécs called on the Yugoslav Commanding Officer, a Colonel Georgevitch, and officially informed him that the Allied authorities had postponed the beginning of the evacuation from August 18 to August 20. The Yugoslav officer gravely replied that, had the Hungarian National Army started its scheduled advance into occupied Baranya on August 18, Yugoslav troops at the line of demarcation would have opened fire.[45]

Where did all this leave Linder and Dobrovits? Apparently the Yugoslav Government had not misled them and had acted in good faith. Belgrade did make a last-minute effort to prolong the occupation, even though it had little faith in the final outcome. This is probably why it gave warning signals to the Baranya Hungarians of the Left between August 6 and 14, the high points of which were Pashitch's offer of August 6 to provide asylum for political refugees; the confidential information given on August 9 that evacuation was impending; and the Yugoslav Interior Ministry's memorandum of August 14 pointing to the near certainty of an evacuation.[46] That Linder and Dobrovits got these signals loud and clear is indicated by their timely preparations to leave Pécs ahead of the scheduled entry of their political antagonists. The continued optimism of Linder's public utterances, even while his wife was already packing,[47] may be explained by a desire not to create panic or perhaps by desperately hoping against hope.

There is no documentary proof that the spurt of Yugoslav diplomatic activity between August 16 and 18 was prompted by the proclamation of the Baranya Republic on August 14 or by the arrival in Belgrade of Rayitch's courier from Pécs with an optimistic report concerning its viability. The pertinent archives of the Belgrade Foreign and Interior Ministries, if they have survived the devastation wrought in Yugoslavia by concurrent horizontal (Yugoslav against Axis) and vertical (Partisan against Chetnik) conflicts during World War II, have not been opened to research scholars. The connection between the last stand of the Pécs Left on August 14 and the Yugoslav diplomatic efforts after August 16 may be only of a questionable *post hoc propter hoc* kind. The possibility of causal connection beyond mere chronological sequence, however, cannot be dismissed after a study of the language of the August 18 Yugoslav note requesting a postponement of evacuation "in view of the events now taking place"[48] in Baranya. This should be interpreted as a rather direct indication of the fact that the Yugoslavs considered their continued presence in Baranya justified by the proclamation of the local mini-republic.

Friday, August 19 was the day of decision for Pécs and Baranya. On that day a new evacuation *démarche* from the Conference of Ambassadors was delivered to the Yugoslav Legation in Budapest.[49] Late in the afternoon Miloyevitch arrived at the Italian Legation, where the

Allied Diplomatic Representatives were assembled in conference in a pessimistic mood. As the Yugoslav diplomat entered the conference room, he wore a smile on his face and spoke mock-heroically: "I have brought peace!" Then he delivered the message from Belgrade: the Government of the SHS Kingdom had consented to the issuance of an order for the evacuation of Baranya, which might start on August 20.[50] In a note, dated the same day, Miloyevitch accordingly informed the Hungarian Foreign Minister, though without giving a date for the beginning of the evacuation, calling attention to the fact that the Allied Representatives had rejected his government's proposal to "adjourn the question of evacuation.[50a] Before the day was over, Colonel Gosset in Pécs invited Hungarian Prefect-Designate Gosztonyi to take over the municipal government from Linder. But the diplomat-mayor could not be found anywhere. In his absence the formality of surrendering the city was performed by the Yugoslav Prefect Rayitch, but only orally, because the stubborn Bachka chauvinist refused to sign the protocol of transfer.[51]

A long weekend was in the offing. Saturday, August 20 was St. Stephen's Feast, the traditional Hungarian national holiday, which this time would be prolonged till Sunday evening. *Munkás (Worker)* published its last number Saturday morning. The final issue announced the end of the occupation, advised against resistance, and recommended "quick flight" from Yugoslav-occupied territory.[52] An exodus of the Left high command and its more immediate followers began at once. Crowds were moving on foot, in carriages, and with pushcarts toward the main railroad station at the foot of *Indóház-utca* (now *Szabadság-utca*) and in the direction of the Üszög suburban depot, where five special Yugoslav trains were awaiting the evacuees. According to a report submitted by Julius Hajdu to Béla Kun in Vienna on September 20, 1921, the refugees included about 700 miners, approximately 1500 industrial workers, 500 additional manual workers from the rural areas; all told about 2700 men with families. Most of these people stayed in Yugoslavia. Only 70 leaders of the Baranya Left continued to Vienna to join the Hungarian émigrés of 1919.[53]

Yugoslav troop withdrawal from the line of demarcation began early Saturday morning, August 20. At the mouth of a Mount Mecsek defile, a retreating Yugoslav and an advancing Hungarian military unit passed each other silently, only the officers exchanging salutes with their sabers. By Sunday afternoon Pécs was without Yugoslav military and civilians. At dusk a patrol of ten Hungarian gendarmes, topped by their characteristic black cock-feathered helmets, marched down *Király* (now *Kossuth*) *utca,* singing the Hungarian national anthem. The following morning advance units of the Hungarian National Army entered the city and mounted a special guard in front of the hotel on Széchenyi Place where their commander, General Charles Soós, was staying. It took five more days for the Yugoslav Army to complete the evacuation of all occupied Hungarian territory north of the new international boundary.

On August 23, while the evacuation was still in progress, French High Commissioner Fouchet reported from Budapest to Paris success for the Allied Diplomatic Representatives' effort to obtain from the Hungarian Government a complete amnesty covering Baranya. The formula of the amnesty was rather curious: there would be no prosecution of persons guilty of crimes committed during the occupation punishable by a maximum penalty of ten years' imprisonment, in the case of which the courts have not rendered sentences exceeding five years.[54] Since the 2000-odd refugees who left Pécs with the Yugoslavs probably included all persons guilty of offenses more serious than those punishable by ten years' imprisonment, Fouchet predicted no reprisals in reincorporated Baranya. He was right. The danger of a military clash, however, persisted until the last moment, as indicated by a rather belligerent note sent by Miloyevitch to the Hungarian Foreign Minister on August 29, in which he spoke disparagingly of Colonel Gosset's role in the evacuation and stated that the Yugoslav occupation forces had been under orders "to repel all attacks." There were no attacks to repel.[55]

Thus, fifty years after the Paris Commune, the microcosmic Baranya Republic passed into history unnoticed by the world, yielding without resistance or bloodshed to the forces of a bourgeois restoration.

Epilogue

The two decisive factors in the prolongation and final solution of the Baranya problem after World War I were Yugoslav resistance to the demands of the military power dominant in the area and the absence of Soviet influence from Middle Europe. In August 1921 the Right was restored in Baranya (as it had already been restored in Hungary proper) because Belgrade was prevailed upon to bow to the superior strategic interests of the Allied and Associated Powers and because, owing to the successful exclusion of Soviet influence from the region, the Pécs Left was dependent for survival exclusively on Yugoslav support. This support could not last indefinitely because, having become a French military theater at the end of the war, the Balkans were subsequently turned into a sphere of French political influence. In his 1921 year-end report from Belgrade the French Military Attaché correctly informed his principals in Paris that "our influence [here] is not only predominant but unique."[1]

At the end of World War II the Right fell from power and was replaced by the Left not only in microcosmic Baranya but also throughout Middle Europe because of a complete reversal of the strategic situation at the continental crossroads. The Soviets now became the military power dominant in the area and succeeded in excluding Western influence from it. In 1944 the northward military offensive in the Balkans which reached and breached Hungary's southern frontier was led by Russian and not by French armies. After a quarter century the dream of the regional Left and the nightmare of the coastal powers came true: Soviet military and ideological power broke out of its containment and filled the Middle European political vacuum created by the collapse of Nazi Germany. The Soviet Army entered Pécs — twenty-three years behind schedule for the Left — on August 29, 1944.

The one historically continuous element in the new Danubian situation, in which leftist governments friendly to Moscow gradually displaced rightist régimes leagued against it, was Yugoslav refusal to subordinate national interests to the strategic demands of the Great Power militarily dominant in the area, now Russian instead of French.

The two old Baranya antagonists, Hungary and Yugoslavia, though both ruled by Communist régimes, respectively received Moscow's seal of approval and disapproval. Historians profited from this partiality because, encouraged by it, the party line no longer called for Hungarian treatment of Yugoslavia with kid gloves. The city of Pécs opened its archives pertinent to the period of Yugoslav occupation and Hungarian survivors of the post-World War I Baranya interlude began publishing memoirs describing the half-forgotten onslaught of Yugoslav *royal* imperialism in 1918–21.

What is the lesson, in a wider historical sphere, of the Pécs[2]-Baranya episode? Does it indicate continuity or change in the relationship between diplomacy and the environment it attempts to shape? If the Baranya dispute and its outcome are to be taken as indicators, the answer is: indeed, more continuity than change.

The ancient *cuius regio eius religio* principle ("he who controls the area, controls the religion"), first articulated in the Peace of Augsburg in 1555, apparently still held in Middle Europe during 1918–1945. The semantic change in the meaning of "religion" from theological to socio-economic belief was subordinate to the persistence of the control principle. As a corollary, the right to emigrate at the moment of change in ideological control, acknowledged in 1555, was still being demonstrated in 1918–1945.

There was also continuity in the traditional diplomatic comportment toward the contingent and the unforeseen. In the possibly paradigmatic Baranya region diplomacy during 1918–1945 still had to accept the *fait accompli* as it had done at Westphalia in 1648, no matter how strenuously it had resisted its generative, anti-hegemonial process. For *faits accomplis,* to which diplomats had to accommodate, were still being created in this part of the globe after both World Wars by the controlling military power which — to quote General Nathan Bedford Forrest — arrived on the scene "firstest with the mostest."

Appendix 1
Sources and Bibliography

The descriptive and narrative parts of this book constitute a greatly abbreviated and selective presentation of the materials contained in the following:

Primary Sources

(a) *Diplomatic.* Documents preserved in the archives of the Ministry of Foreign Affairs, Paris, catalogued as follows:

Série Z 746 I — Yougoslavie Nº 17

Télégramme du 28 mars 1919
Lettre du Ministre des Affaires Etrangères au President du Conseil, Ministre de la Guerre (4 avril 1919)
Lettre de l'Attaché Militaire en Serbie au Ministre de la Guerre (1 octobre 1919): "Aperçu sur les armées serbes"
"Démobilisation de l'armée serbe," 24 mars 1920
Rapport du Lieutenant-Colonel Delteil au Ministre de la Guerre, Belgrade, 23 decembre 1921

Série Z 751 Dossier 4 — 1921 — Serbie Nº 63

Feuillets I-36, 55–76, 77–85, 93–132, 132–134, 135–184, 196–216, 241–262

Série Z 751 Dossier 4 — 1921 — Serbie Nº 64

Feuillets 31–44, 48–53, 60–86, 184–185, 200–206

Documents published in Hungary, Ministry for Foreign Affairs, *Papers and Documents Relating to the Foreign Relations of Hungary,* edited by Francis Deák and Dezső Ujváry, 2 vols., Budapest, 1939 and 1946.

Documents stored in Great Britain, Public Records Office, London.

Treaty text printed in Fred L. Israel (ed.), *Major Peace Treaties of Modern History, 1648–1967,* 3 vols., New York, 1967.

Military convention text printed in Harold W. V. Temperley (ed.), *A History of the Peace Conference of Paris,* vol. 1, London, 1920.

(b) *Parliamentary.* Debates printed in

Great Britain. *Parliament. House of Lords.* The Parliamentary Debates (Official Reports). Fifth Series, vols. XLIV–XLV, London, 1921.

Hungary. *Nemzetgyűlési Napló* [National Assembly, Parliamentary Record], vols. X, XI, and XII, Budapest, 1921.

(c) *Administrative.* Documents and studies printed in

Pécs. Municipal Council. Executive Committee, Cultural Division. *A Magyar Tanácsköztársaság Pécsi-Baranyai Emlékkönyve* [The Pécs-Baranya Book of Memories of the Hungarian Soviet Republic], Pécs, 1960.

Hungarian Socialist Workers' Party. Baranya County Committee. Propaganda and Education Division. *Időrendi Áttekintés a Pécs-Baranyai Politikai Eseményekről, 1919–1921* [Chronological Survey of Events in Pécs-Baranya, 1919–1921], Pécs, 1966.

Hungarian Socialist Workers' Party. Baranya County Committee. Propaganda and Education Division. *Baranya Megye 1919-ben* [Baranya County in 1919], Pécs, 1969.

Baranya County Council. County Library. *Baranya és a Forradalmak: Pécs és Baranya 50 Évvel Ezelött a Helyi Sajtó Tükrében* [Baranya and the Revolutions: Pécs and Baranya 50 Years Ago in the Mirror of the Local Press], Pécs, 1969.

Márton Vörös, *Az 1919–1921. Évek Baranyai Dokumentumainak Sorsa. A Magyar Tanácsköztársaság Pécsi-Baranyai Emlékkönyve.* [Fate of the Baranya Documents of 1919–1921. Pécs-Baranya Book of Memories of the Hungarian Soviet Republic], Pécs, 1960.

In this essay a former Pécs archivist relates his fruitless search in Yugoslavia (Subotica and Belgrade) for administrative documentation removed from the Pécs City Hall on August 20, 1921 by Yugoslav military transport and shipped to Yugoslavia. See especially pp. 186–187.

(d) *Memoirs*

Gyula Hajdu, *Harcban Megszállók és Elnyomók Ellen* [Fighting Occupiers and Oppressors], Pécs, 1957.

Documented recollections of a Pécs Socialist leader and eye-witness to the events of 1918-1921.

Károlyi, Mme Michael, *Együtt a forradalomban* [Together in the Revolution], Budapest, 1967. Diary and recollections of the wife of the President of the First Hungarian Republic.

Correspondence with Mr. Milorad M. Drachkovitch, son of Milorad Drashkovitch, Yugoslav Minister of Interior during the Baranya occupation.

Correspondence with Lt. Gen. (ret.) Kálmán Hardy, Hungarian Army. As a Lieutenant Gen. Hardy served as liaison officer with the Allied Moore mission in Pécs in 1920.

Secondary Sources

(a) *Diplomatic.* Francis Deák, *Hungary at the Paris Peace Conference,* New York, 1942; Ivo Lederer, *Yugoslavia at the Paris Peace Conference,* New Haven and London, 1963; Zsuzsa L. Nagy, *A Párizsi Békekonferencia és Magyarország, 1918-1919* [The Paris Peace Conference and Hungary, 1918-1919], Budapest, 1965; Alfred D. Low, *The Soviet Hungarian Republic and the Paris Peace Conference,* Philadelphia, 1963; Arno J. Mayer, *Politics and Diplomacy in Peacemaking, 1918-1919,* New York, 1967.

(b) *Political.* Rudolf L. Tőkés, *Béla Kun and the Hungarian Soviet Republic,* New York, 1967; Alex N. Dragnich, *Serbia, Nikola Pašić and Yugoslavia,* New Brunswick, N.J., 1974; Stephen Graham, *Alexander of Yugoslavia,* New Haven, 1939; V. S. Mamatey and R. Luža (eds.), *History of the Czechoslovak Republic, 1918-1948,* Princeton, 1973; Marcel de Vos, *Histoire de la Yougoslavie,* Paris, 1965; Leslie C. Tihany, *A History of Middle Europe,* New Brunswick, N.J., 1976.

(c) *Local History.* Imre Dankó, *Pécs Képekben* [Pécs in Pictures], Pécs, 1967; János Kolta, *Pécs,* Budapest, 1967; Márton Vörös, *Pécs,* Budapest, 1942.

(d) *Lexical Aids. Révai Nagy Lexikona* [Révai's Great Lexicon], Budapest, vol. II (1911) and vol. XV (1922); *Bolshaya Sovietskaya Encyclopediya,* Moscow, vol. IV (1952); *Magyar Életrajzi Lexikon* [Hungarian Biographic Lexicon], Budapest,

1969; *Munkásmozgalom-Történeti Lexikon* [Lexicon of the History of the Workers' Movements], Budapest, 1972; Zoltán Gombocz and János Melich, *Lexicon critico-etymologicum linguae Hungaricae,* vol. I, Budapest, 1914; H. Lauterpacht (ed.), *Oppenheim's International Law,* vol. II, London and New York, 1944; William L. Langer, *An Encyclopedia of World History,* Boston, 1940; Neville Williams, *Chronology of the Modern World,* New York, 1967; Péter Gunst (ed.), *Magyar történelmi kronológia* [Hungarian Historical Chronology], Budapest, 1968; L. C. Wickham Legg and E. T. Williams (eds.), *The Dictionary of National Biography, 1941–1950,* Oxford, 1959; and *The Statesman's Year-Book,* New York, 1975.

(e) *Bibliographic.* Paul L. Horecky and David H. Kraus (eds.), *East Central and South-East Europe: A Handbook of Library and Archival Resources in North America,* Clio Press, Joint Committee on East Europe Publications, Series 3, Santa Barbara, California, 1976.

For additional monographs and articles see FOOTNOTES.

Appendix 2
Selected Documents

Appendix 2-A

Conference of the Allied Representatives and Generals, Sitting of February 26, 1921.

Procès Verbal

Hearing of Major Dérain, French Army, Interallied Military Mission at Pécs.[1]

Having welcomed Major Dérain, *the President* asks him to present the situation at Pécs, where he has been on assignment for more than a year.

Major Dérain notes that from the very beginning the Pécs occupation has shown a character contrary to the rules of occupation as laid down at The Hague. In fact, shortly after the arrival of the Serb troops, the Prince Regent issued a decree ordering that for the duration of the occupation the territory occupied should be considered as constituting a part of Serbia and that Serb laws should be applicable therein. The Hungarian civil servants were placed under obligation on penalty of expulsion to swear [allegiance]. Having refused to do so, the majority had to leave in the face of such particularly hard conditions. They have been replaced by Serb civil servants of the SHS state.

In fact, there is no *military occupation* but a takeover by civilian authorities who get their orders from [are dependent upon] the Ministry of the Interior.

The SHS government collects the taxes and exercises all the state rights [of governing] without assuming any obligations. The roads are not maintained; the hospitals and other public services are not receiving the subsidies to which they are entitled.

---

[1] Translation from the French original.

The President asks if the salaries of the Serb civil servants are provided from the taxes collected.

Major Dérain explains that the Serb government has established a Baja-Baranya-Bácska section, which belongs to the Ministry of the Interior, with civil servants coming mostly from Croatia. The few civil servants of Serb origin do not occasion too many complaints, but those of Croatian nationality commit all sorts of abuses. They were chosen because of their familiarity with the country, but do not measure up to their task, and want to prove their patriotism by indulging in zealous excesses, which manifest themselves by an inadmissible tyranny.

The President asks if, from the administrative point of view, there is any difference between the territories temporarily occupied and those definitively ceded to Serbia.

Major Dérain replies that Serb laws are applied everywhere, equally in both, although in the Hungarian territories Hungarian laws should be applied and that only the Serb *military* authorities should exercise power alongside with the local civilian authorities. But, completely to the contrary, [Hungarian civil] authority had to yield entirely to the civilian authorities installed by the occupier. Passports are visaed by the Serb civilian authorities, which refuse to recognize permits of travel even when issued by the Serb military authorities. Perhaps these abuses are beyond the intentions of the SHS government and it seems that in Belgrade they are unaware of the true situation. An employee of the Ministry of Justice who recently visited Pécs was quite amazed by what he saw and promised to enter the field in Belgrade against the Communists installed at Pécs.

Major Dérain stresses the fact that the Pécs municipality is strictly Communist and is affiliated with the Third International. Béla Linder, who personally is not an extremist, remains at the head of the municipality. He had threatened to retire in January, the Serb government having refused [to desist from] levying exorbitant taxes of a Bolshevik character. But the government yielded before this threat and the prefect obtained for [Linder] a promise of 4 million Serb crowns. By a curious coincidence the first payment was made on the very day that the SHS government undertook measures in Belgrade against the Communists.

Prince Castagnetto asks if the SHS government is not concerned about the presence of Communists at Pécs.

Major Dérain thinks that the Communists are kept in power mostly by the local authorities. The [SHS] civil servants want to keep their jobs and are looking for all means possible to prevent an evacuation, which would leave them without employment. Consequently, their tactics appear to consist of provoking troubles in the area and of engaging in blackmail aimed at the Conference of Ambassadors, who, they hope, will not dare to demand the end of an occupation which has been presented to them as the sole guarantee of order in this country. For these [SHS] civil servants the sole question is staying on the job and preventing the execution of the treaty by all means possible, because obviously on the day the treaty enters into force the Prince Regent's decree, which now sets the conditions of the occupation, will become invalid and the occupied territory will have to be returned to Hungary.

For the moment the line of demarcation is a closed barrier and no commerce whatsoever is permitted between the occupied territory and the rest of Hungary. This is a particularly inadmissible consequence of the present state of affairs.

Prince Castagnetto inquires about the status of railroad communications with Hungary and wishes to know if it is really true that rails have been removed at various points.

Major Dérain replies that in several places rails and fixed equipment have indeed been lifted and removed. Major Dérain could not protest to the [SHS] civilian authorities, whom he considers irregular, for fear that by entering into relations with them he would provide them with the occasion to turn the matter to their advantage by raising their standing through an implied recognition extended by the representatives of the Entente. He therefore had to be content with protesting to the military commander, Colonel Cholak-Antitch. The latter, who as a matter of fact no longer has any authority, has not responded to [Dérain's] protests.

As regards the railroad traffic, *Major Dérain* explains that it has completely stopped.

The President would like to know how taxes are collected.

Major Dérain indicates that, as far as this point is concerned, the occupier's proceedings have been especially vexatious. Over and above excessive taxes for the current fiscal year, taxpayers had to pay taxes a second time for 1917 and 1918.

Most recently the occupier has decided to collect anew taxes on war profits for the years 1914, 1915, and 1916 already paid to the Austro-Hungarian Treasury, amounts of which were arbitrarily tripled. Thus, a taxpayer assessed 400 crowns for 1914, was forced to pay 1,200 crowns in Serb crowns (whose value is four times that of the Hungarian crown), so that [the man] ended up by disbursing nearly 5,000 crowns to settle a tax liability of 400 crowns which he had *already paid* in 1914. Major Dérain presents to the Conference a tax assessment addressed to a taxpayer by the Serb authorities, which proves irrefutably the abuse committed by the SHS authorities.

The President inquires concerning the manner in which justice is dispensed.

Major Dérain explains that, in principle, the Hungarian judges have retained their functions but they are powerless. As soon as they have to deal with an offender who belongs to the socialist party, the regular [process] of justice is abandoned and the case is brought before the tribunal of the Border Police, which is not impartial. Recently a Hungarian subject was murdered by policemen who threw him out of the prison window. The case caused a great scandal, but still the investigation was assigned at first to a regular judge, who ordered the arrest of the guilty [parties]. One of these, a Hungarian subject and a former murderer who had been freed from prison at the time of Béla Kun's *coup d'état* and [then] entered the service of the Pécs Police, fled. As for the other [guilty party], also a Hungarian subject, City Prefect Rayitch objected to his being tried and claimed that his case would be placed before Serb judges who were supposed to come from Serbia for this purpose. Since Major Dérain protested against such an abuse of power, the prefect simply had the guilty [person] released. The latter has left town and gone to Serbia.

Prince Castagnetto asks Major Dérain to enlighten [the Conference] regarding the exploitation by the Serbs of the forests belonging to the Széchenyi family. The Conference has had to take up this matter on several occasions. As a last resort the Serb government alleged that because the Széchenyi family had entered into a contract with the Austrian Treasury for the exploitation of these forests, the Serb authorities, to whom the rights of the Austrian Treasury had been transferred, were entitled to carry out the contract. Prince Castagnetto reads a letter signed by Counts Géza, Anton, and Frederic Széchenyi, in which these latter [three] present themselves as a delegation opposing the claims made by the Serb authorities. They had never entered into a contract with the Austrian government; they had only dealt with a [commercial] firm named Kenkel of Pécs.

Major Dérain reports that information in his possession confirms the declaration made by Messrs. Széchenyi. He has frequently visited the location and found that exploitation of the forests was a fact. He has protested to the Serb military command. Colonel Cholak-Antitch admitted that the exploitation was illegal but said it would continue. The SHS government will pay for the damage caused and will leave it for the Reparations Commission to fix the amount.

General Mombelli is of the opinion that recourse should be had at once to the Reparations Commission, so that it may at a later date have the facts needed to make a decision.

Major Dérain states as a fact that in the case of the forests belonging to Count Géza Szechenyi, exploitation has ended.

General Mombelli asks if one should say exploitation or destruction.

Major Dérain opines that the term destruction is in fact more appropriate. At first the Serbs had planned exploitation of the large trees, which they needed to make railroad ties and telegraph poles. At present they are pillaging everything and are cutting down trees barely grown. They have set up local workshops, where the timber is cut into planks and is processed. The result is that when they [now] remove a trainload of lumber, [the load] represents a far more considerable swath cleared than in the beginning when timber was removed in a raw state. The Major adds that he will submit a detailed written report on the timber removed.

The President asks Major Dérain whether in his opinion the owners of the forests are within their legal rights.

Major Dérain replies that in his opinion there is no doubt whatsoever regarding their [legal rights]. He adds that no other question should draw the attention of the Conference [as much] as that of the sequestrations. A great number of properties has been irregularly sequestered. In addition, the Serb authorities have made use of the right of requisitioning in the most arbitrary manner, removing at their convenience cattle, horses, agricultural produce, machinery, and a large share of the harvest. This year the requisitioning of the harvest will be still more complete because the SHS government has dispatched to the localities agents who are at work preparing the operation [of requisitioning].

Prince Castagnetto expresses the opinion that Paris should be informed of the necessity to finish [this business] before the harvest.

M. Fouchet thinks that it would be useful to submit a comprehensive report on the question.

Prince Castagnetto shares this opinion. The danger of requisitioning at harvesting time and the Bolshevik danger should be reported.

Major Dérain thinks that these two dangers should indeed draw the attention of the Conference.

Certainly, due to the experience the Serb authorities have had and the measures they have carried out [in this matter], they will in all likelihood confiscate the entire harvest.

As for the Bolshevik danger, Major Dérain thinks that this is a real threat. [In Pécs] one is in a den of veritable Communism. The Socialists, who have repudiated the descriptive title "Social Democrat" [of their party], are affiliated with the Third International. The party has divided the city of Pécs into 13 districts. In each of these districts meetings take place every Thursday, real Communist meetings, which are corrupting the population.

At Siklós the Serb vice-prefect has established a school of "political education." Women, children, and young people attend to take veritable lessons in Bolshevism. Every Sunday more important gatherings are held. The population comes carrying red flags; at one of these meetings the vice-prefect delivered a speech praising the Lenin régime.

Nearly all employees of the Pécs municipality have revolutionary antecedents. Among them about 30 are former agents of Béla Kun or leaders of the red army. The number of refugees coming from Vienna has assumed alarming proportions. For the most part these are men who had fled Hungary when the Communist régime fell. They have founded a club which has an incontestable political importance, especially in view of the fact that the leaders are energetic men who will stop at nothing.

The Serb government subsidizes all these disorderly elements and in January permitted a payment of 4 millions to them. A part of this sum has already been effectively disbursed. Major Dérain thinks that the SHS government had no positive knowledge of for whom this sum was destined, the Prefect Rayitch having indeed asked for it foi [the use of] the hospitals, which are state hospitals. The prefect, [however], transmitted the money to the municipality, which is making use of it for propaganda purposes, and has paid to the hospitals only a ridiculously small sum [and that only] after protests.

The President recalls that the Conference has already looked into the lamentable situation of the hospitals, which have been forced to discharge their patients for lack of nourishment to feed them.

Major Dérain notes that the SHS government, while it tolerates or arranges these abuses at Pécs, represses Bolshevism in its own territory.

Prince Castagnetto would like to have Major Dérain prepare a comprehensive report on the Pécs question for the use of the Conference of Ambassadors.

General Mombelli proposes to Major Dérain that he extend by a few days his sojourn in Budapest and draft his report [here]. During this time Capt. Mando could stay alone at Pécs.

The President suggests that Major Dérain should be sent to Paris to be heard in person by the Conference of Ambassadors. A few minutes of direct contact produce better results than the best-written reports.

Prince Castagnetto is of the opinion that the Conference of Ambassadors should be asked first whether it would accept such a suggestion.

The President expresses the opinion that action is needed. The situation is grave. There is a treaty whose application the Allies demand but whose obligations they fail to fulfill. A treaty is a bilateral obligation and for the Allies it is a matter of justice not to shrink their obligations.

M. Fouchet shares this opinion.

The President adds that this matter of justice is coupled with a veritable danger, against which one must ready himself.

Major Dérain agrees with this assertion and says that, in fact, the danger is pressing. First he had been an optimist and in the beginning had thought that it was merely a question of agitation by extremist elements but not Communists. The situation has completely changed during [the past] 8 months and one is [now] faced with real Communism. The arrival of several Russians coming from Constantinople might render the situation even more grave. From the moment of their arrival the Socialist Party invited them to sign up [to become members] with promises of money and jobs.

Major Dérain has tried to blunt the blow by establishing an employment office. But his work was made difficult by the fact that there are many officers among the refugees. Even so, these [officers] are satisfied with modest jobs as bottle washers and watchmen. Besides, all these Russians are of fairly good mettle, but in their straitened circumstances one has to fear that they will allow themselves to accept the offers of the Socialists, who are trying to win them over.

The Major cites the case of two Russian engineers who went to ask the City Engineer, a certain Lippich, for employment. The latter asked them if they were Communists. Upon their negative reply, he threw them out, saying: "There is nothing for you here — Go home to fight the reds!"

The Bolsheviks are no longer in hiding and are aware of being supported. The censorship permits publication of all their articles but does not allow the newspapers of the other parties to reply. This is a veritable Communist dictatorship. Béla Linder has been overtaken and left behind.

The President asks who is the brain of this Bolshevik organization.

Major Dérain repeats that it is not Béla Linder, who is at the mercy of extremist elements. He did attempt to resist but to no avail. For a few days he did not even go to the city hall. He has been violently attacked by the extremists and is no longer supported by the Serbs because he is opposed to the annexation of the occupied area to the SHS state.

Also, the Serbs would like to replace him by a certain Polácsi, a person of the most dangerous kind, founder of the Thursday meetings, who may be considered as chief of the Communists.

Among the other leaders of the movement one must cite a certain Hajdu, who was deported by the Serbs some time ago because he refused to help them carry out their plans. He is an extreme Socialist, of Hungarian nationality, who left Budapest after the fall of Béla Kun. He is supposed to go to Riga to take part in the negotiations with the Soviets for the exchange of POW officers for former people's commissars [now] under sentence.

Another influential personality is Dr. Doktor, who used to be engaged in revolutionary agitation in Italy, from where he has returned to Pécs.

The President thanks Major Dérain for the explanations he has given. He asks him upon what conditions the members of the missions might be able to visit Pécs in a personal capacity.

Major Dérain believes that such visits would be inconvenient because they would probably lead to approaches on the part of the Serb civilian authorities. By entering into relations with [the latter] one would run the risk of giving them a chance to take advantage [of the contact] by boasting of [having won] recognition from the Entente. As far as he is concerned, he has avoided any and all relations with these irregular civilian authorities and will have contact only with the commander of the occupation troops.

Appendix 2-B

Report of the Socialist Party of Pécs-Baranya To The Third Congress Of The Communist International. (Draft Dated June 10, 1921).[1]

The Belgrade Armistice Agreement drew the line of demarcation between the Hungarian and Serb armies as a straight line connecting the towns of Baja-Pécs-Barcs, permitting these towns to be occupied by the Serb army. The occupation took place within a short time. Hungarian armed formations were disarmed and the civil administration of the entire territory was taken over by the Serb authorities. Only over the city of Pécs was the old Hungarian administrative organization retained.

The Peace Treaty of Trianon designated the Hungarian national frontiers farther to the south. According to this treaty, only a very small territory belongs to Yugoslavia in the angle of the Danube and Drava rivers, while the so-called Baja Triangle, situated in Bács County, as well as the larger part of Baranya County, including the towns of Pécs, Mohács, and Siklós, in addition to Szigetvár and Barcs in Somogy County, remain in Hungarian territory. The area between the two boundaries has a population in round numbers of 300,000, of whom 210,000 are Hungarians, 70,000 Germans, 8,000 Serbs, and 12,000 of other Slavic nationalities.

This geographical zone, which is to be returned to Hungary, is one of that country's most fertile areas. Eighty-two per cent of the soil is arable land, the rest forest and pasture. As regards land distribution and cultivation, c. 60% [of the soil] consists of large estates over 500 cadastral *holds* [1 Hungarian *hold* = 1.4 acres], so that almost two-thirds of the area constitute estates owned by almost 40 proprietors.

In the environs of Pécs there are anthracite coal mines which employ about 5,000 miners. The normal output of the mines is a daily 220–240 wagonloads of anthracite coal. In addition, other larger industrial plants are: porcelain, leather, machinery, beer, furniture, brick and cement factories. The number of industrial employees in the entire

---

[1] Translation from the Hungarian original.

territory is 35,000, of whom 25,000 fall to the share of the factory industries.

2. The territory of Pécs-Baranya is, therefore, juridically a part of Hungary; in reality, however, it is under Yugoslav military and civil governance. All connections toward Hungary have been severed; [the area] may not maintain any legal contact [with Hungary] either politically or economically.

The Yugoslav governments have done everything possible to obtain recognition of this territory as belonging to them, and have still not given up the hope of annexing it for themselves. Apart from the desire for expansion natural to imperialism, they cling to this territory for military and economic reasons.

Militarily it is important for them to maintain the present boundary because it is a natural frontier marked by the spine of Mecsek Mountain and therefore strategically the best line of defense. On the other hand, the frontier delineated by the Treaty of Trianon runs along a pair of railroad tracks, without supporting points of defense.

Economically the coal mines lend a special significance to the territory. There is no mining of anthracite coal anywhere else in Yugoslav territory, and there is a great shortage of brown coal also. Although the Peace of Trianon gives an option to the Yugoslav state on about one-half of the yield of the Pécs mines as compensation for the destroyed Serb mines, the Yugoslav governments are aware that, in the event of an evacuation, the option would only be of an illusory value. This springs from the fact that, except for this [area], the Hungarians also have only insignificant anthracite coal mines; therefore, in spite of the provisions of the treaty of peace, [they] would probably not surrender any of the yield. Furthermore, it is not to be doubted that, should the mines return to Hungarian rule during the Horthy régime, a goodly part of the miners would emigrate, so that coal production would decrease greatly.

In the face of Yugoslav strivings, one of the most frequently mentioned questions of Hungarian public life is the reacquisition of Baranya. In consequence of the Treaty of Trianon Hungary has lost two-thirds of her territory; she is therefore doing everything to get back this section of the country which, according to the peace treaty, is hers. Hardly a week passes without interpellations in the Budapest parliament regarding the return of Baranya; and, after several target dates announced and passed, the government is now declaring that, in the course of the compliances following the ratification of the Peace of Trianon, it will win back this territory.

This area is, therefore, a constant point of friction between Yugoslav and Hungarian strivings. The Belgrade government has taken the position that it is under obligation to comply only if the Hungarians have carried out all provisions of the peace, including the evacuation of West Hungary and disarmament. Additionally, they have issued an official statement that they will maintain the occupation as a collateral to assure that the Habsburgs will not return to the Hungarian throne.

Both sides have addressed the Supreme Council of the Entente in order to make their positions prevail, but no measures worth mentioning have yet been taken by that body.

The question of this territory's return will no doubt be resolved with the clarification of the relationship between the Little Entente and Hungary. This alliance is directed against Hungary and includes [as one of its points] Yugoslav occupation [of Baranya]. If, on the other hand, negotiations conducted by the intermediary Czechoslovak government should prove to be successful, one of the prime requirements of the Hungarian government will certainly be a reacquisition of Baranya.

Since Pécs is one of the most important industrial towns of Hungary, the political and economic organizing of the workers saw its beginning here decades ago. Before the war the Social Democratic Party had here its strongest organization after Budapest; while the National Federation of Miners grew to nationwide proportions from an organization of the Pécs miners.

During the final years of the war the party in Pécs was able to hold demonstrations involving great movements of the masses. After the victory of the Russian proletarian revolution, it swung even more decisively to the left, in a revolutionary direction. The Serb occupation took place at the beginning of the Károlyi revolution. [The occupiers] tried to oppress all workers' movements, resorting to martial law proclamations, until finally the workers of Pécs won recognition for the freedom of their organizations by means of a general political strike lasting three weeks.

The establishment of the Hungarian Soviet Republic signalled an important turning point for the working masses of Pécs as well. The Serb commandaturas did everything they could to seal off the occupied territory from Soviet Hungary, but failed completely. The workers abandoned the mines and the factories *en masse* and, fleeing across the line of the occupation, reported to the Hungarian Red Army. Seven battalions were formed from the workers of this territory, who bravely stood their ground till the last day of the Soviet

Republic. In the meantime, in the mines occupied by the Serb imperialists, the production of coal had practically come to a stop, since the workers were fighting for the cause of the proletariat.

After the fall of the [Hungarian] Soviet Republic, the formation of a Hungarian Social Democratic government did not for a moment mislead the miners of Pécs. They started discussions with the Serb authorities and, having been guaranteed their immunity from punishment and freedom of movement, they marched in closed ranks to their former places of employment, surrendering their arms to the Serbs and not to the Hungarian white commands.

4. Even after the fall of the [Hungarian] Soviet government, the workers of Pécs-Baranya kept up their revolutionary spirit. The Social Democratic leadership of Budapest vainly attempted to win over the local workers; each time it met with the most determined refusal. The trade unions separated from the yellow federations of Budapest and formed their own federations. As for the party, it operated under the name of "Socialist Party," contentwise in accordance with the guidelines of the Third International.

After the troubled situation following the collapse, the trade unions got back on their feet very quickly. Almost without exception, the workers of the mines and factories are members of their trade unions, which number 15,000 members, while in the environs, where the number of industrial workers is limited, the agrarian proletarians of many communes — especially those who speak German as a mother tongue — group themselves in agrarian workers' trade unions. The number of organized workers in the environs is 8,000.

In the tradition of the old Social Democratic system, every union member is at the same time member of the political party. But the action of separating has started and since several months special party organs have entered the process of administrative formation. Their operations are, however, still in an incipient stage.

The party is publishing a daily newspaper entitled MUNKÁS [Worker], which at this time appears in 10,000 copies. In addition to it, there are Hungarian- and German-language weeklies for agrarian workers, a miners' union paper, and a paper for young workers. All these are edited in a Communist spirit. The same is true of the education of the workers. The weight of the Social Democratic elements is negligible. These do not participate in the party leadership.

5. The jurisdictional situation peculiar to Pécs-Baranya has created a distinct situation in the political strivings of particular classes.

The Hungarian government has done everything to organize in the occupied territory an irredentist movement as strong as possible, in order to compel in this manner the occupiers, through the use of internal forces, to a quick evacuation. And since the overwhelming majority of the population consists of Hungarians, there is a fertile soil for irredentist action.

The strongest supporters of the Horthy system in this territory are the civil servants. These have been either removed from their positions by the Yugoslavs or must live in fear of being removed from them; they receive their salaries from the Hungarian government, for the most part through illegal channels, and for this reason they are the most natural supporters of irredentist strivings. The economic interests of the employers are better satisfied under Yugoslav rule, because marketing is easier and the foreign currency has a higher value. During the time of the Hungarian Soviet Republic they consequently tried everything to make the occupation final; since the conclusion of the Treaty of Trianon, however, being aware of a return to Hungary sooner or later, they are attempting everything to qualify as protégés and not victims of the Horthy armies when these march in. The financial institutions and the industrial plants are competing with one another in sabotage, so as to create an economic situation in which the workers will be constrained to wish for a Hungarian rule. They are outbidding one another in order to become as worthy as possible of the Hungarian counterrevolution, whose arrival is expected with certainty from week to week.

The landowners are also promoters of irredentism, since in Yugoslavia they would have to be on their guard against a serious land reform. For nationalistic reasons one part of the peasantry is also in the camp of irredentist strivings, but is not susceptible to activism; another part is content with the exploitation of daily advantages and remains completely passive.

Not for a moment, however, could the workers be led astray by irredentist action. White agents, internal as well as from Hungary, have tried everything to infiltrate the workers' ranks but the workers made clear their position with solid unanimity: Horthy-Hungary is not their fatherland and they will do everything to avoid being brought under its yoke.

Action taken by the Socialist Party had two directions: it was designed to serve both local and national objectives. Locally the work of the party was directed toward uniting the workers in occupied territory in the camp of the conscious flagbearers of the class struggle. And since it became obvious that, in the event of an entry of the Hungarian white forces, the workers would fall victim to unprecedented blood-letting, the party designed its policies so as to prevent the return of this territory to Horthy-Hungary. As regards the national point of view, [the party] strove to make use of this area, which provided more free-dom and possibility for agitation, as a base for the resuscitation of the Hungarian working class and for the struggle against the Hungarian counterrevolution.

The party endeavored to serve both objectives by means of huge demonstrations involving 20–30,000 workers, by agitation covering the whole territory, and by seeking contact with the working masses in Hungary. In these actions the strength of the party swelled powerfully; the self-awareness and revolutionary readiness of the workers in-creased beyond a doubt.

On numerous occasions the workers turned for help to the Yugoslav authorities against the irredentistically-motivated, sabotaging capital-ists, at times not without success. In the face of irredentist agitation these [Yugoslav authorities] also recognized the common interest and because of this, the occupiers did not raise obstacles to action against the Hungarian counterrevolution.

Finally the party's strivings took a concrete form: [the party] raised a demand for autonomous jurisdiction for the occupied territory, while maintaining a Serbian military occupation until such time as a regime guaranteeing organizing and political freedoms for the workers should come to power in Hungary. In essence autonomy would have been placed under the party's influence as well as direction and would have been an opportunity for the organization of an avant-garde to lead the overthrow of the Hungarian counterrevolution.

The Belgrade government did not refuse the party's demand, but in reality it allowed elections only for assumption of the administration of Pécs. As a result of the elections the party took control of the municipal administration, though without guarantee of whatever jurisdiction.

The party committed a serious political mistake when, in such circumstances, it took over the municipal administration, and even more so when it continued to carry on after the situation became obvious. The Serbs got rid of the old city leadership, which was in the service of irredentism and of annoyance to them; yet they did not provide the new leadership with an opportunity to take action con-sonant with the intentions of the working masses and capable of having an effect in Hungary also.

The municipal administration contributed to the rise of a bureaucratic camp, which looked on its administrative position as a self-contained goal. The city government should have been an instrument in the service of party objectives; instead of this, the bureaucracy endeavored to debase the party into its own instrument in order to retain its position.

6. In the eyes of the workers respect for the party was strongly undermined by a municipal administration without jurisdiction. They could not discern even an attempt to realize social strivings. Economic movements, especially those of the miners, were systematically suppressed by the municipal bureaucracy — at the request of the occupying authorities — for [reasons of] higher policy. Thus, the strength of the party, until recently respected on every side, was greatly dissipated: the confidence of the workers was jolted, the Serb authorities considered [the party] as their instrument, while the economic crisis, which was increasing during the turmoil, continued to strengthen the irredentist camp.

These circumstances evoked the rise of several factions within the framework of the party. Not infrequently these fought against one another with the most desperate means though without clearly formulated slogans.

One of the camps is being led by the bureaucracy which has found positions in the city government. These are mostly émigrés, for whom the objectives of the party and socialism itself are completely alien [concepts]; their only interest is to remain in their positions as long as possible. For this reason they constantly keep on inventing new and often contradictory justifications for the acceptance of their opportunistic points of view and behavior. And since, by the use of clever tactics, they have been able to place actual proletarians in the administration, they utilize these [proletarians] as instruments for winning over certain groups of workers.

The manipulators of another faction are without doubt in the pay of the Serb authorities. Certain Serb politicians are of the opinion that, in the event they are successful in prevailing upon a part of the local workers to demand openly an annexation of this territory to Yugoslavia, they would be able to bring around the entente [powers] to a recognition of the annexation. To reach this goal they have been able to win over morally weak individuals, mostly émigrés, who engage in agitation for this concealed objective. They cannot declare annexation [as their goal] because the workers react to all such strivings with the greatest revulsion, knowing that the furtherance of imperialist interests, whether Serb or Hungarian, is a betrayal of the working class.

Accordingly, they flaunt Communist slogans, sound calls to revolt, endeavor to recruit a following by means of revolutionary romanticism, and attempt to embroil in a putsch certain individuals or groups in the expectation that by so doing they will bring about a situation in which Hungarian rule would be tantamount to danger of life for as many workers as possible, and thus personal fear would render [such workers] recruiters for the annexionist camp.

There is a third faction, which is motivated by revolutionary impatience and by a mistaken interpretation of Communist tactics. They orate about the ultimate goals of Communism and brand as traitors all those who have not come out for a declaration of the dictatorship of the proletariat within [the next] ten minutes. They deride the struggles of certain economic organizations as well as secondary actions of lesser significance; they dissolve the unity of militant workers, weaken their strength, because always and everywhere there are workers who "fall" for leftist slogans and, in order to avoid being considered opportunists, betray the cause of Communism in the belief that they are serving Communist [objectives].

However, the majority of the party has retained its original position. Instead of a constant chorus of Communist slogans and the dictatorship of the proletariat, it endeavors to strengthen Communist consciousness in the masses; it keeps awake their revolutionary spirit; while it honestly struggles to find a solution for daily problems in the interest of realizing economic strivings. Since it sees clearly [the nature] of the turmoil caused by the way in which the city is governed as well as the opportunism born of it, it wants to see the party independent of the bureaucracy, have the [members] fend for themselves, [reserving] full freedom of action [for the party] vis-à-vis both the occupying power and the city leadership.

The empoisoned rivalry among the various factions is creating constantly increasing trouble. The influence [of the factions] has led to a negative rather than to a positive orientation. Many have been swept into the arms of the "leftists" or even of the annexionist agents due to loathing caused by the bureaucrats' opportunism. On the other hand, those who clearly recognized the motivation behind the militancy of the latter, sought refuge in supporting the opportunists.

The organizational errors and shortcomings explain why trouble could develop to this point.

7. After the second congress of the Communist International, the party accepted the 21 points and so informed the Communist Party in Yugoslavia, stating that it wished to work with [the CPY] in good

understanding. No organizational liaison was, however, set up with the party in Yugoslavia; such [liaison] would not be conducive to a practical purpose. As Hungarian-speaking workers employed in *de jure* Hungarian territory, the party in Pécs-Baranya desired organizational liaison with the Communist Party in Hungary, but this succeeded only to a small degree.

During August last year, at the party's demand, the Yugoslav authorities gave permission for the return of Comrade Julius Hajdu, leader of the Pécs party for a decade, in emigration since the fall of the Hungarian dictatorship. Comrade Hajdu came to Pécs as a delegate of the Communist Party in Hungary, and directed the party's local activities according to principles agreed upon with the party's central committee. Principal guidelines were: (1) harmonious cooperation with the party in Yugoslavia within political and economic movements; (2) the building of autonomy subject to the party's influence, and, if this should not be possible; (3) keeping the party at a distance from the organizationally impotent city government dependent [for its existence] on the good pleasure of the Serb political and military authorities. The first goal was fully accomplished; the realization of the second and/or third objectives was prevented by the fact that, upon his return, Comrade Hajdu found a *fait accompli*. Action accordingly began against the opportunist elements and, since the events occurring fully justified the Communist stance, the party decided during December no longer to accept the municipal administration. The Yugoslav authority responded by expelling Comrade Hajdu, and after his departure the opportunists ensconced in the city administration succeeded in persuading the party to postpone the implementation of the decision.

An untold amount of trouble and collision sprang from this. In the eyes of the working masses the party was responsible for the mistakes in carrying on the city's business, and the party leadership sensed the awkward character of its position, and yet the central committee of the Communist Party in Hungary neglected, after the departure of Comrade Hajdu, to look after [party] direction in a different manner, and thus the masses were placed at the mercy of the scheming intellectuals who were clinging to their positions.

Although the central committee of the Hungarian party paid some attention to Pécs as an area of illegal activity directed toward Hungary, it did not, on the other hand, maintain contact during this time with the working masses in spite of repeated requests from the latter, nor did it provide systematic political direction for their benefit. This resulted not only in the disadvantage that the movement [led by] the Pécs party could not, for lack of direction and guidance, mesh with the general movements, but also in giving occasion for the in-rushing émigrés [to exploit] the increasing despair of the masses facing the opportunists, by causing more complications with on-the-spur-of-the-moment, individual action, which ultimately led to a distortion of [the workers'] clear vision. More than one [émigré] were able to gain credibility for their actions by [referring to] instructions from the central committee of the Hungarian party; though all [acted] in a manner so as to conceal under a cloak of Communist slogans their various real objectives. It is without doubt that, should the Communist Party in Hungary have given appropriate guidance and effected intervention, all this could have been avoided.

8. A clear analysis of the given situation and of the positions taken by the various party factions makes it manifest what should be the correct comportment to be followed in the future.

This territory, being an object of rivalry between Yugoslav and Hungarian imperialisms, the party's task is to deepen as much as possible the contradictions between the [two] embattled imperialisms and to produce between them [increasingly] more frequent and sharper clashes. [The party] must fight energetically against both Hungarian irredentist and Yugoslav annexionist strivings, and must unmercifully expose the agents of both. For the Pécs workers the success of the Hungarian irredentist movement would mean a massacre, an unprecedented revenge of the Hungarian white terror. As for a Serb annexation, it would bring in its wake the same oppression of the workers under which the working masses of Yugoslavia suffer in their entirety.

The proletarian masses must be enlightened that a liberation of the working class is possible only through a proletarian revolution. But just as it is the duty of every proletarian to attempt everything to make sure that the preconditions of civil war will follow [and that] he should be ready for the combat, so should one condemn every self-styled, leftist, slogan-juggling orientation, which, by a constant voicing of the ultimate goals [and] perhaps by the mounting of ill-timed actions and putsches, distorts the workers' clear vision and, in the final analysis, as a result of easily [foreseeable] fiascos, weakens their faith in the revolution.

The influence [exerted by] the municipal bureaucracy on the party is to be eliminated most energetically. The party cannot tolerate that the masses should be strengthened in a belief that the fiascos of the municipal administration result from the party's program and not from measures taken by the occupying authorities as well as from the incompetence of the bureaucrats.

It is correct to preach autonomy at a time when [by so doing] there is hope for a postponement of the entry of Hungarian rule. It is correct also because it is suitable to drive a wedge between embattled imperialisms. But if it should come to a realization [of autonomy], nothing must be surrendered from the real objectives of the party for the sake of creating a new bureaucracy. In such an organizational unit there could be participation by unexposed elements of the party even if in unison with bourgeois elements, but the proletarian elements must not be kept or left in error even for a moment that, from the party's point of view, such an organization is not a goal but only the means to promote the revolutionary readiness of the workers and to make possible the recruitment of an avant-garde to bring about the triumph of the Hungarian revolution. But every striving toward allowing the bureaucracy of a possibly autonomous status [to become] master of the party must be nipped in the bud. On the contrary: it is the party which must at all times keep the bureaucracy under its own influence.

The party should get involved most energetically in the economic struggles of the trade unions; [such struggles] should be generalized and deepened according to the necessities of the situation.

The party continues to operate as a socialist party. It is the duty of every Communist to work in the party and for the party; every attempt at party division is to be rejected most energetically.

Special tasks will fall to the lot of the party in the event of an evacuation of the occupied territory. A transition must be carefully prepared lest the entry of white troops should automatically signal a dissolution of the party. The party's daily newspaper, the MUNKÁS, is to be strengthened and an editorial staff is to be readied which will be able to continue the editorial work under possible Hungarian rule. Even after the evacuation the party should remain a socialist party; it should reject probable approaches by the Budapest Social Democratic center and guard its separateness, so that as a party of the masses it might serve as a starting point for the future Communist Party in Hungary.

9. Organizationally the Pécs Socialist Party is part of the CPH. Locally a party leadership is formed to conduct local policy, keeping in mind general guidelines and extending a helping hand to the CPH or its commissioners in order to facilitate actions directed toward Hungary. For the purpose of eliminating the influence of the bureaucracy, it should be proclaimed as a principle that members of the party

leadership and of the control committee may not accept municipal or similar offices. The party leadership is in direct contact with the executive committee of the national party. In the structuring of the CPH organs, the wishes of the Pécs party, [which] for the time being is the only mass party, are to be taken into consideration.

The local party organs are to be built up, strengthened, and readied for the [eventual] independence of the party organs from the trade unions. Party organs must be built up also in the provinces, in the villages, so as to make possible the beginning of vigorous agitation among agrarian proletarians and semi-proletarians.

In addition to the legal party the cadres of an illegal party must also be formed. Reserves should exist for the eventuality of an evacuation of the occupied territory. Illegal party cells must be trained in every plant, every trade, and in every party organ from trustworthy comrades of a communist persuasion, and these [cells] should be brought into an organic form of interdependence. Émigrés are not to be admitted into such party cells, and from among the local workers only such [persons] who, in the event of an evacuation, will foreseeably not emigrate. After the evacuation this illegal organization will take over operations. Its duties will be, on the one hand, the maintenance of the proletarian movement; and, on the other, a counterbalancing of influence [exerted] by Social Democratic or independent elements. It is also the duty of this illegal organization to start preparing everything as of now, so that in the event of an evacuation the party should be able to function as effectively as possible in constructing the Hungarian front of the class struggle.

June 10, 1921

Appendix 2-C

Despatch from M. Fouchet, High Commissioner of the French Republic in Hungary, To H.E.M. Aristide Briand, President of the Council, Minister of Foreign Affairs; Budapest, August 23, 1921.
Subject: Evacuation of Baranya by Yugoslav Troops.[1]

At the hour I am writing these lines, the evacuation of Hungarian territory occupied by Yugoslav troops continues in a normal manner, pursuant to the program outlined by the Allied representatives at Budapest, assisted by Allied generals. Since this evacuation presented certain difficulties, I believe I should sum up here the events of the last several days.

For some time prior to August 18, the day originally set for the evacuation, it seemed to me that, without having revealed its secret intentions, the SHS Government showed little haste in responding to certain demands of the Allied governments, for example, regarding the subject of designating a sole military Commander with whom alone the Interallied Military Mission in Baranya should be able to establish contact so as to facilitate matters. When news was received by my colleagues and by me that the Cabinet of Belgrade had finally designated in fact not one but two military chiefs to preside over the evacuation of the territories, we noted it with pleasure in spite of the relative imperfection of this decision. But almost at the same time, on August 14, we received a communication from British Colonel Gosset, Chairman of the Interallied Military Commission in Baranya. This communication informed us that even though the Belgrade Government had acknowledged receipt of the Allied Governments' notice that the evacuation should start on the 18th, it reserved for itself [the right] to fix subsequently the date of the evacuation, which Serb civil servants stated could not take place, in any event, in less than three months. At the same time, about 4,000 Communists, assembled in the [main] square of Pécs, proclaimed the independent Republic of Baranya. M. Rayitch, the irregular Serb civilian prefect, was reported to us by Colonel Gosset as the [moving] spirit of this manifestation.

---

[1] Translation from the French original.

On August 16 M. Miloyevitch, the Serb Minister at Budapest, brought to our attention verbally and by a succession of letters that (1) in view of the obvious desire of the population to oppose a return of the Hungarians, his government stood in fear of bloody complications; (2) having considered this state of affairs, the Cabinet of Belgrade considered as indispensable a postponement of the evacuation of Baranya until a later date. He asked additionally certain economic guarantees in advance, notably the exploitation by the Serbs of the railroad line from Pécs *via* Villány to the Serb frontier. According to him these conditions had to be complied with in a completely satisfactory manner before everything else.

My colleagues and I did not remain inactive in the face of these maneuvers and of such notorious bad faith. Step by step our Conference reported by telegram to the Conference of Ambassadors on August 14, 16, and 18 the disquieting turn events might take. At the same time [the Conference] declared by collective letters to the Minister of Serbia in courteous but very energetic terms that the date August 18 had to be kept for the evacuation of Baranya because [postponement] threatened to delay the transfer of the [West Hungarian] Counties to Austria; that it was in fact impossible to demand that Hungary unilaterally comply with the Treaty; and finally that, as regards the question of the economic guarantees [so] abruptly raised at the last moment, the Allied ministers at Budapest were not competent to resolve [the matter]; and that the program, stopped with the agreement of the Powers, now had to be scrupulously carried out. We added that, since the evacuation of Baranya could no longer start on the 18th, that of the [West Hungarian] Counties would in its turn not begin until the 23rd instead of the 21st. Colonel Gosset had been kept up-to-date by us regarding these negotiations. Being in agreement with us, he informed the Serb Colonel Georgevitch that the initial [military] operations had been postponed from the 18th to the 20th. The situation remained quite disquieting as indicated by the fact that Serb Colonel Georgevitch told Colonel Gosset on the 18th that had the Hungarian troops begun their advance on that date, the Serb troops would have opened fire.

While this was happening, the Minister of Serbia arrived on the evening of the 19th to call on my colleagues and me at the Italian Legation, at the exact moment we had just dispatched him the note received [that] afternoon from the Conference of Ambassadors, which invited the Serb Government [to undertake] an immediate evacuation of the territories. M. Miloyevitch told us, with some humor and with visible satisfaction, that he came to bring us peace and that, faced with such a formal desire of the Entente, his government had finally consented to order evacuation. This [operation] might therefore begin on the 20th. Until today no incident worth reporting had occurred, [he said]. If everything goes as expected, [the evacuation] should be completed on the 27th instead of the 25th. It had been agreed that after the evacuation Serb Lt. Colonel Ititch would remain at the disposal of the Hungarian authorities for three more weeks, with a view to smoothing over all litigous cases which might yet arise pursuant to the withdrawal of the Yugoslav troops.

During these rather anxious days spent [in observing] Serb resistance, Hungarian concern, the worry of the Austrian Minister over too much delay in the transfer of the [West Hungarian] Counties, and finally the ever-present eventuality of a bloody outcome, the Magyar government displayed *sang froid* [as well as] submission to our will, so that even in the circumstances it could still look after its interests; but, far from raising a thousand questions and details, as is its custom, it acted in a flexible manner and did not hesitate to give us satisfaction as regards a guarantee requested by the Serb government, the only one we had retained of the demands presented by M. Miloyevitch at the last minute. I refer to the guarantee concerning persons accused of Communism, intended in all probability to become objects of prosecution by the Hungarian government. It is true that the latter had already prepared, in advance, a proclamation on this subject, which on the whole was rather vague. Since it always behooves us to be a bit distrustful when it comes to carrying out verbal assurances given by the Magyar authorities, we called on the Cabinet of Budapest [to issue] an ordinance decreeing a complete amnesty. We have obtained one for persons guilty of crimes punishable by a maximum of 10 years' imprisonment, upon whom the courts have not passed a sentence in excess of 5 years. This formula is rather curious and elastic, and is indicative of the complicated Magyar mentality. We have nevertheless found it adequate, since in this manner almost all Communists, with the exception of the leaders, will be in a position to escape punishment, which might have been terrible. What's more, 2,000 Communists, evidently the most guilty ones, may already have fled. There is thus reason to hope that the retaliation envisaged will be practically nil.

Since operations have not yet terminated, one should be on one's guard against considering all difficulties as definitely overcome. Some may still arise before the very last moment. But today complete success seems probable. The principal consequence [of success] will be a compensation, which the Hungarians will certainly appreciate, for the cession of the [West Hungarian] Counties to Austria, and it is fitting, it seems to me, to rejoice in this, for the internal condition of this country and for the peace of mind [of the population]. We should also congratulate ourselves that the Yugoslav government could finally, though regretfully, comprehend the situation. The fact that my colleagues and I delayed the transfer of the Counties by two days due to the resistance put up by Belgrade against the restitution of Baranya, played no small part, I believe, in convincing the Serb Cabinet. The note of the Conference of Ambassadors arrived at the right time to confirm very fortuitously the results which thenceforth we could rightly consider as having been accomplished.

(signed) M. Fouchet

Appendix 2-D

Report of Julius Hajdu to Béla Kun, Sept. 20, 1921[1]

Vienna, Sept. 20, 1921

Dear Comrade Kun:

The day before yesterday I received your kind letter of August 30, in which you refer to several previous letters. Of all these only one communication has reached me, to the effect that the newspaper would be supplied with newsprint. Unfortunately, this has become immaterial in the meantime.

The party held a congress mid-June. The agenda included a setting forth of the party's political guidelines and election of the leadership. The overwhelming majority of the delegates certified at the congress were of the communist persuasion, expecting instructions from the central committee regarding their comportment. For your information, the party delegates sent to Pécs, Farkas and Komor (the latter being the young workers' well-chosen secretary), came to Vienna for a discussion of the Pécs situation and were supposed to take back a reply. But, although they arrived three weeks in advance, they were asked to stay on here day after day [with the assurance] that they would be receiving directives in just one more day. The result of several weeks' waiting for these "instructions" was that the congress took place without them. In consequence, it was the annexionists who orated at the party congress, hidden under a communist cloak, and their role was most dishonorable. They let fly a few revolutionary phrases. As for the most pressing question — that concerning City Hall — they passionately belabored the municipal leadership without presenting theoretical objections, with the ultimate intention of replacing the Linderites in their offices. In order to justify this striving in the eyes of the Serbs, they (Dr. Fekete and his companions) made a motion before the congress to convey its thanks to the Serb government commissioner for his democratic treatment of the workers' movements. In their great enthusiasm they were not restrained by the fact that, but a week before, this same government commissioner had

---

[1] Translation from the Hungarian original.

ordered MUNKÁS ["Worker"] to dismiss the communist members of its staff or else he was going to close down the paper. Nothing was more natural, therefore, than that a section of the less class-conscious proletarians — due to being dished out this kind of stuff in the name of communism — turned away from this clique and, for want of a better center of attraction, made common cause with the Linderites. After the congress an impassioned electoral agitation started, as a result of which the right-wing list peddled by the trade union leaderships got the majority.

It was during the days of the election that the party delegates finally arrived, bringing with them the article entitled "Pécs" I had written for PROLETÁR as far back as last May. This article was an exposé of the annexionist camp and of the Linderites. Results came quickly. The annexionist clique — a few intellectuals and associated émigrés — was isolated. The miners and the trade union masses, one after another, declared themselves, demanding that the policy indicated in the article should be followed. The largest trade unions were at the point of meeting and voting no-confidence in the party leadership which was following Linder's policies. The movement had just begun to be reoriented in the right direction when lightning struck — news came of the evacuation.

Despair and bitterness overwhelmed the Pécs masses, which had constantly been misled into believing that the Serb government had promised to continue the occupation. When finally the press announced even the date of the transfer, the Linder crowd fell silent and would not give a word of instruction about what was to be done. The party leadership stood impotent and in its final convulsions made Wommert (then in Moscow) party secretary. The Linderites at once denounced him to the Serbs as a participant in the Comintern Congress, whereupon he was arrested and tortured. But by then Wommert had convoked the party to a mass meeting scheduled for August 14, which therefore had to be held. The official leadership issued no slogans for the mass meeting; they repeated the usual phrases about Horthy, the white terror, etc. Then, unexpectedly, at the end of the meeting, Dr. Fekete, the exponent of the annexionists, declared that there was only one solution, proclamation of the Baranya Serb Republic, and immediately had the meeting swear allegiance to the republic. The surprised crowd, hoping thus to escape a Hungarian occupation, enthusiastically agreed, swore the oath, and demonstrated, raised on their shoulders Peter Dobrovits, the exponent of the Serbs, who declared himself President of the executive committee.

Very characteristic is a comment made in my presence by Tivadar Pobuda (former municipal councillor in the capital) and the moving spirit of the Linder group. The proclamation of the republic — he said — came just in the nick of time, because the masses had become so embittered and depressed that, without having this development as an outlet for their emotions, they might have massacred the men of City Hall.

This remark, I believe, has a lot of truth to it, because everybody could see and sense the catastrophic bankruptcy of Linder's policy, which had built everything on the Serbs.

At this juncture Linder himself was in Belgrade. Upon being informed of the events over the telephone, he stated that he unconditionally approved the proclamation of the republic, would participate in its government, and would remain [in Belgrade] to await the arrival of Dobrovits and Gábor Schwarz (a Pécs attorney), Linder's strongest follower), who were already on their way to Belgrade to discuss the matter further.

But the workers of Pécs were not for a moment misled regarding what was happening. The Trade Union congress, previously scheduled, convened on this same day. At the invitation of the Linderites, Deputy Brkits was in attendance, the worst specimen of scum from the South Slav Social Democratic Party. He delivered a great oration in Hungarian at the congress and wound up saying that they [the Social Democrats] were willing to take steps in the interest of continuing the Serb occupation, but the congress should declare that the party accepted without reservations the position of the Second International and expressed as its sense that the policy of revolution was in error. The delegates of the Trade Unions (in other words, the farthest rightist elements of the crowd) booed him down and declared that they were not willing to carry on discussions in such a sense.

As for Linder in Belgrade, like so many times before, he made the rounds of the ministerial waiting rooms, and returned to Pécs in the evening of August 18. There at once he held a meeting, at which he stated that Premier Pashitch had made a concrete promise that there would be no evacuation. One hour later appeared the announcements of the government commissioner making public the hours of train departures on the following day for those who needed transportation to flee. The refugees started on five special trains, about 700 miners and 1500 workers from Pécs, and an additional 700 from the countryside. In Yugoslavia the government saw to their relocation and employment, so that the overwhelming majority settled there. Only 70 comrades came up to Vienna. Many of these would be eminently suitable for party work, but all my urgings to this effect have so far been of no avail. It is certain, however, that the Yugoslav refuge will not last longer than a few months, because they [the refugees] are completely at the mercy of the local authorities and persecution has already begun in certain towns. We are slowly reestablishing contact with these comrades. Regarding those who stayed behind, it will take a few weeks before we shall be able to handle them again. No organization remained after the evacuation because during the final struggles everybody lost his cover and consequently everybody capable of action had to flee. After the entry of the Hungarians, the persecution of the workers began but about this we still lack precise information.

With comradely greetings,

Julius Hajdu

Pécs, Széchenyi Place with Trinity Monument.

103

Pécs Cathedral (11th – 19th centuries).

Street Scene, Pécs.
105

Street Scene, Pécs.

Baranya County Building, Pécs.
107

Main Entrance, Baranya County Building, Pécs.

108

Pécs University Library.

Old Town, Pécs.

Workers' Dwellings, Pécs.

Tettye Resort, Mecsek Mountain, with ruins of 16th-century episcopal summer palace. City of Pécs in the plain below.

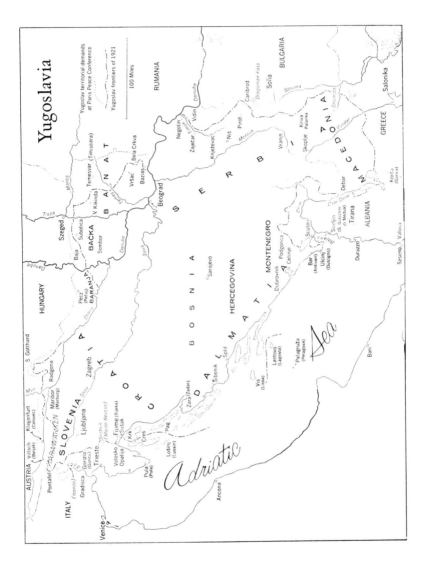

113

MAP I.

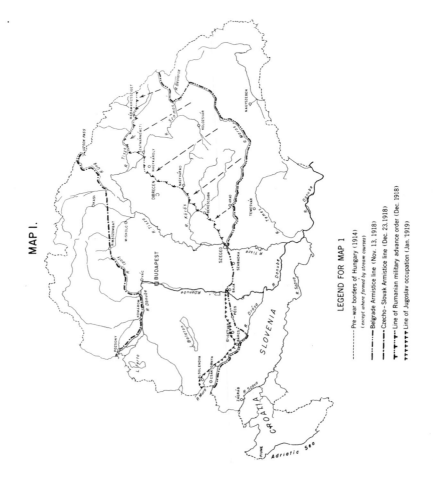

LEGEND FOR MAP 1

-------- Pre-war borders of Hungary (1914)
    (except where formed by stream courses)
▬▬▬ Belgrade Armistice line (Nov. 13, 1918)
▬·▬·▬ Czecho-Slovak Armistice line (Dec. 23,1918)
▼▬▼▬▼ Line of Rumanian military advance order (Dec. 1918)
▼▼▼▼▼▼ Line of Jugoslav occupation (Jan. 1919)

114

MAP 2.

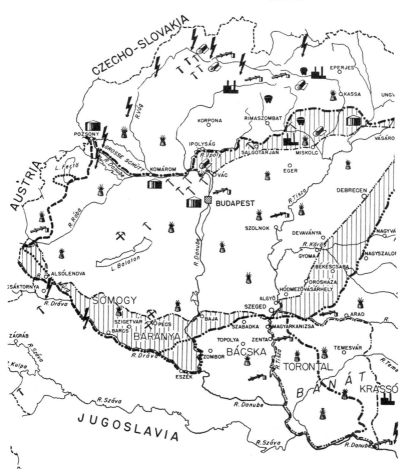

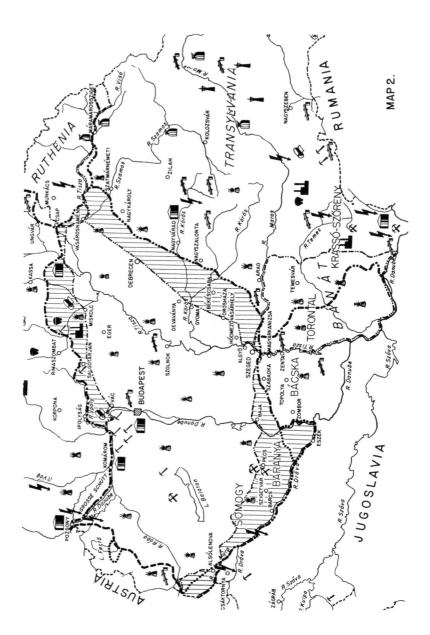

MAP 2.

116

Appendix 5
Chronology
Of Internal and External Events
Pertinent to the History of Baranya,
1918–1921

May 20, 1918	Regimental Mutiny in Pécs
June 15–24, 1918	Austro-Hungarian Piave offensive fails
October 17, 1918	Ex-Premier Tisza tells Hungarian Parliament: "We have lost the war."
October 30–31, 1918	Bourgeois-democratic revolution in Budapest. Pécs joins revolution.
November 1, 1918	National Council established in Pécs
November 3, 1918	Austria-Hungary signs Padua Armistice
November 13, 1918	Hungary signs Belgrade Military Convention.
November 14, 1918	Serbian Army enters Pécs
November 16, 1918	Hungary proclaimed independent People's Republic
November 20, 1918	Communist Party in Hungary established
December 1, 1918	Kingdom of Serbs, Croats, and Slovenes proclaimed (SHS).
December 3, 1918	Pécs National Council protests SHS intention to detach Baranya from Hungary
December 22, 1918	Christian Socialist Party established in Pécs

1919

January 5–15	Spartacist uprising in Berlin

January 20	SHS military command expels Budapest-appointed prefects from Baranya. Belgrade-appointed prefects in control.
January 30	SHS military command expels Mayor Nendtvich of Pécs from occupied area
February 22–March 13	General strike in SHS-occupied Hungarian territory
March 2	Comintern is founded in Moscow
February–March	Communist uprisings in Germany
March 20	Károlyi government resigns in Budapest
March 21	Hungarian Soviet Republic (HSR) proclaimed
March 26	HSR decrees socialization of all industrial, mining, and transportation enterprises employing more than 20 persons
March 29	HSR socializes all educational institutions, including parochial schools
April 1	SHS military command permits return and resumption of office of Pécs Mayor Nendtvich
April 3	HSR collectivizes all large- and medium-size landed estates
April 4–May 1	Soviet Republic in Bavaria
April 4	Gen. Jan Christiaan Smuts visits Budapest on fact-finding mission
April 16	Rumanian Army crosses Belgrade Military Convention line into Hungary
April 27	Czechoslovak Army crosses line of demarcation into Hungary
May 1	SHS military command in Pécs bans Labor Day celebration
May 9–20	Hungarian Red Army launches offensive against Czechoslovak forces
May 18–March 2, 1920	War between Rumania and Soviet Russia
June 1	Allied ultimatum demands Hungarian Red Army withdrawal from Slovakia

June 13	Second Allied ultimatum demands evacuation of Slovakia
June 16	Hungarian offensive reaches Preshov (Eperjes). Slovak Soviet Republic proclaimed.
June 24	Brief military uprising by cadets and gunboat crews against HSR in Budapest
June 30	Hungarian Red Army starts general retreat from Slovakia
July 24–30	Rumanian Army crosses Tisza River and marches on Budapest
August 1	Hungarian Soviet Republic falls. Government of Trade Unions takes over
August 3	Rumanian Army enters Budapest
August 7	Rightist *putsch* in Budapest removes Trade Union government
September 1	SHS military command permits public meeting of Social Democratic Party (SDP) in Pécs
September 30–October 12	Allies evacuate Archangel and Murmansk
November 14–16	Rumanian Army evacuates, Hungarian National Army under Admiral Horthy enters Budapest.
November 30	Allied fact-finding mission under US Lt. Col. Moore arrives in Pécs

1920

January 1	Strikes in Pécs
January	SHS military command arrests former Hungarian army officers as conspirators in Pécs
January 15	Hungarian delegation in Paris receives preliminary draft of peace treaty
January 15	SDP quits Hungarian government and announces boycott of forthcoming elections

January 25–February 13	Smallholders Party wins Hungarian elections
February 17	Two leading SDP journalists are murdered by White Terrorists in Budapest
February 26	SDP mass meeting in Pécs calls for continued SHS military occupation
March 1	Hungarian National Assembly elects Admiral Horthy Regent
March	Spartacist insurrection in Ruhr territory
March 15	Workers' mass meeting in Pécs asks for prolonged SHS occupation and declares itself in favor of Comintern
March 16	Conservative-monarchist Albert Apponyi protests White Terror to Hungarian parliament
March 21	SHS military command permits commemoration of Hungarian Soviets' first anniversary in Pécs
April	Yugoslav Communists announce affiliation with Comintern
April 25	War between Poland and Soviet Union
May 1	SHS authorities in Pécs permit Labor Day celebrations and demonstrations for Comintern
May 4	Hungarian delegation in Paris receives final text of peace treaty
May 28	Interallied Military Commission (IMC) is established in Pécs
June 4	Treaty of Trianon between Allies and Hungary is signed
June 10	Pécs Socialists complete report for Comintern on Baranya situation
June 12	Pécs SDP changes name to Pécs Socialist Party (SPP) to indicate Comintern orientation

June 13	SPP mass meeting calls for continued SHS occupation
June 27	Pécs middle-class organizations petition IMC for end to SHS occupation
July 27	Soviets invade Poland
August 8	SHS authorities permit reestablishment of National Council in Pécs
August 9	British Laborites prepare for general strike in the event of Soviet-British war
August 14	Red Army at gates of Warsaw
August 14–17	Little Entente of Czechoslovakia, Rumania, and Yugoslavia formed
August 29–30	SPP wins municipal elections in Pécs
September 22	SHS authorities expel (for second time) Pécs Mayor Nendtvich from occupied territory
September 23	Béla Linder, former member of Károlyi government, installed as Mayor of Pécs
October	SPP declares adherence to Comintern
November 10	Premier Teleki of Hungary orders arrest of White Terrorists
November	Civil War in Russia ends in Soviet victory
November 21	SPP expels pro-annexionist leader Polácsi
December 19	Protests in Pécs Municipal Council against SHS administrative interference
December 24	SHS authorities expel anti-annexionist SSP leader Hajdu from occupied territory

1921

| January 8 | Pécs Mayor Linder meets Yugoslav Interior Minister Drashkovitch to discuss autonomy for Yugoslav-occupied territory |

February 8	SPP organizations in Baja and Mohács secede from Pécs center and ask Belgrade for autonomy
February 27	Pécs workers demonstrate against their employers and ask Yugoslav authorities to nationalize certain factories
March 8	French troops occupy (until September 30, 1921) Ruhr coal basin of Germany
March 26–27	Ex-King-Emperor Charles fails in his *putsch* to reoccupy Hungarian throne
April 27	Conference of Ambassadors informs Belgrade it will have to evacuate non-treaty occupied territory upon ratification of Hungarian peace treaty.
May 1	SHS authorities permit mass celebrations of International Labor Day in Baranya
May 3	Conference of Ambassadors informs Belgrade it should start preparations for Baranya evacuation
May 29–June 1	Trade Union Congress in Pécs
June 28	Attempt on Prince Regent Alexander's life in Belgrade
July 13–22	Miners strike for higher wages in Pécs coalfields
July 21	Yugoslav Interior Minister Drashkovitch is assassinated
July 26	Convention is signed establishing International Commission of the Danube
July 30	Belgrade journal *Epoca,* identified with Premier Pashitch, denies early possibility of Baranya evacuation
August 1	Law Concerning Public Security and Order in the State is passed by Belgrade *skupshtina;* Communist deputies are expelled; Communist Party is outlawed
August 4	Pécs Mayor Linder and Prefect Rayitch

are received in Belgrade by Interior Minister Pribichevitch

August 6   Yugoslav Premier Pashitch promises Linder asylum for all Baranya political refugees in the event of evacuation

August 8   Yugoslav *skupshtina* permits arrest of eight expelled Communist deputies

August 9   Yugoslav government confidentially informs Linder of impending Baranya evacuation

August 11   British Colonel Gosset arrives in Pécs to head Interallied Military Commission charged with supervising evacuation

August 12   One-day protest strike in Pécs against evacuation

August 13   Yugoslav Prefect Rayitch issues communiqué: "reports of impending evacuation are without reliable foundation"

August 14   Rayitch transmits to Mayor Linder Belgrade memorandum concerning probability of evacuation

August 14   Trade Union Conference meets in Pécs

              Baranya Republic is proclaimed in Pécs

August 15   Prefect Rayitch sends news to Belgrade by courier and pledges support

              Baranya Republic Executive Committee calls on British Colonel Gosset to protest evacuation; envisages sabotage

              Mohács, Szigetvár, Siklós, Barcs and Baja adhere to Baranya Republic

August 16   Belgrade asks for postponement of evacuation and economic guarantees both in Budapest and Paris

August 18   Yugoslav Legation in Paris asks Conference of Ambassadors for evacuation delay

August 19	Allied evacuation démarche to Yugoslavia
	Belgrade informs Allies and Hungarian Government it will start evacuating on August 20
	Colonel Gosset calls on Hungarian Government Commissioner in Pécs to accept transfer of city. Rayitch performs transfer orally.
August 20	Yugoslav evacuation starts. Exodus of about 2000 leftist families.
August 21	Hungarian gendarmerie patrol enters Pécs
August 22	Hungarian National Army units commanded by Gen. Charles Soós enter Pécs
August 27	Yugoslav Army completes evacuation of all Hungarian territories occupied since 1918 north of new international boundary.

Appendix 6
Footnotes

Abbreviations: In citing the major sources listed under Appendix 1, the following abbreviations will be used in the footnotes: *FFAA* (French Foreign Affairs Archives) for the unpublished archival materials microfilmed in the Archives of the Ministère des Affaires Etrangères, Paris; *FRH* (Foreign Relations of Hungary) for the documents published in Hungary, Ministry for Foreign Affairs, *Papers and Documents Relating to the Foreign Relations of Hungary,* edited by Francis Deák and Dezső Ujváry, 2 vols. (Budapest, 1939 and 1946); *EK (Emlékkönyv)* for the documents, abstracts, and studies appearing in *A Magyar Tanácsköztársaság Pécsi-Baranyai Emlékkönyve* [The Pécs-Baranya Book of Memories of the Hungarian Soviet Republic] (Pécs, Municipal Council, 1960); and *Hajdu* for the memoirs and documents published in Gyula Hajdu, *Harcban Elnyomók és Megszállók Ellen* [Fighting Oppressors and Occupiers] (Pécs, 1957). Less frequently used sources will be cited in full, with abbreviation given, the first time they appear in a chapter. Diplomatic documents will be cited with names of sending and receiving persons or agencies stated, date given, and place of origin mentioned whenever significant.

Introduction

1. The place name *Baranya* (pronounced Ba'ranya) first occurs in writing in 1141. It is probably derived from Slavic *brana,* gate, gateway. See Zoltán Gombocz and János Melich, *Lexicon critico-etymologicum linguae Hungaricae* (Budapest, 1914–1930), vol. I, columns 282–284. Imre Dankó, *Pécs képekben* [Pécs in Pictures] (Pécs, 1967), p. 36, derives the word from a personal name, that of the first *ispán* (province chief) of this region. (Henceforth Dankó.)
2. The place name *Pécs* (pronounced Paytch) first occurs in writing in 1093 and is open to etymological speculation. The most likely origin of the word is Old Slavic *pest,* kiln, oven. See Dankó, p. 33 and János Kolta, *Pécs* (Budapest, 1967), pp. 16–22.
3. Great Britain. *Parliament. House of Lords.* The parliamentary debates. (Official Reports). Fifth Series, vol. XLIV (London, 1921), column 682.
4. Admiral Nicholas Horthy (1868–1957), Regent of Hungary, 1920–1945.
5. Yugoslavia did not become an official country name until 1929. Between 1918 and 1929 the country now referred to as Yugoslavia was officially

known as the Kingdom of the Serbs, Croats, and Slovenes (abbreviated SHS). Prior to 1918 the central part of the SHS Kingdom had existed as Serbia. During the period covered in the following pages, all three names — Serbia, Yugoslavia, and SHS — were used interchangeably though only the last-named officially. Their inhabitants were referred to both as Serbs and Yugoslavs. In this book the terms Yugoslav and Yugoslavia will be used preferentially, though not exclusively, as most capable of carrying meaning at this writing. In Baranya during 1918–1921 the occupying forces and authorities were commonly referred to as Serbs.

6. *Munkásmozgalom-Történeti Lexikon* [Lexicon of the History of the Workers' Movement] (Budapest, 1972), p. 53.

Chapter I

1. *Révai Nagy Lexikona* [Révai's Great Lexicon] vol. II (Budapest, 1911), pp. 586–588 (henceforth Révai); *Bolshaya Sovietskaya Encyclopediya* (Moscow, 1952), IV, p. 228.

2. Révai, vol. II, pp. 586–588.

3. *Ibid.*

4. *Ibid.*

5. *Ibid.*

6. *Ibid.*

7. *Ibid.*

8. *EK* (see *Abbreviations*), p. 47.

9. Révai, vol. XV (Budapest, 1922), "Pécs."

10. *Ibid.*

11. *Ibid.*

12. *Ibid.*

13. Leslie C. Tihany, *A History of Middle Europe* (New Brunswick, 1976), Chapter I.

14. *Ibid.*

15. Révai, vol. II, pp. 586–588.

16. *Ibid.*

17. Imre Dankó, *Pécs képekben* [Pécs in Pictures] (Pécs, 1967), pp. 38–40 (henceforth Dankó); János Kolta, *Pécs* (Budapest, 1967), pp. 42–46.

18. Hajdu (see *Abbreviations*), p. 20.

19. *Ibid.*, p. 15.

20. *Ibid.*

21. *EK,* p. 34.

22. *Ibid.*

23. Hajdu, p. 34.

24. *EK,* p. 36; Hajdu, p. 103.

25. *EK,* p. 37; Hajdu, p. 37; Rudolf L. Tőkés, *Béla Kun and the Hungarian Soviet Republic* (New York, 1967), p. 227.

26. Hajdu, p. 166.

27. *Ibid.*, pp. 21–22.

28. *Ibid.*, p. 16.

Chapter II

1. *EK* (see *Abbreviations*), pp. 38–39; Hajdu (see *Abbreviations*), pp. 197–205.
2. *Ibid.*
3. For the text of the Belgrade Military Convention of November 13, 1918 see Harold W. V. Temperley (ed.), *A History of the Peace Conference of Paris,* vol. I (London, 1920), pp. 491–493. Although the document signed at Belgrade and printed by Temperley is generally known and often referred to as the Belgrade Armistice, strictly speaking it was a Military Convention which made provision for a cessation of hostilities and for a post-hostilities order of things in the Hungarian parts of the Austro-Hungarian Monarchy. See Alfred D. Low, *The Soviet Hungarian Republic and the Paris Peace Conference* (Philadelphia, 1963), p. 14, and Zsuzsa L. Nagy, *A Párizsi Békekonferencia és Magyarország, 1918–1919* [The Paris Peace Conference and Hungary, 1918–1919] (Budapest, 1965), pp. 9–16.
4. Hungarian Socialist Workers' Party, Baranya County Committee, *Baranya Megye 1919-ben* [Baranya County in 1919] (Pécs, 1969), p. 5.
5. Peter Pastor, "The Vix Mission in Hungary, 1918–1919: A Re-examination," *Slavic Review* XXIX.3 (1970), pp. 481–498.
6. Mme. Mihály Károlyi, *Együtt a forradalomban* [Together in the Revolution] (Budapest, 1967), pp. 303–304, 466–467.
7. Leslie C. Tihany, *A History of Middle Europe* (New Brunswick, 1976), Chapter XX.

Chapter III

1. See footnote 3, Chapter II above.
2. Péter Gunst (ed.), *Magyar történelmi kronológia* [Hungarian Historical Chronology] (Budapest, 1968), p. 319 (henceforth Gunst).
3. See footnote 7, Chapter II above.
4. *EK* (see *Abbreviations*), p. 49, and Hajdu (see *Abbreviations*), p. 208.
5. *EK,* p. 97; Hajdu, p. 213.
6. Hajdu, p. 213.
7. *EK,* pp. 91–98.
8. *Ibid.*
9. Hajdu, p. 212.
10. *Ibid.*
11. See footnote 4, Chapter II above, pp. 5–59.
12. Hajdu, p. 217.
13. Imre Dankó, *Pécs képekben* [Pécs in Pictures] (Pécs, 1967), p. 98.
14. See conversation between Hungarian Foreign Minister Count Teleki and Yugoslav diplomatic representative Miloyevitch, reported by the Hungarian Ministry for Foreign Affairs to the Hungarian diplomatic representative in Belgrade on September 29, 1920, in *FRH* (see *Abbreviations*), vol. I, p. 652.
15. On The Hague Regulations (referred to as the Second Hague Convention in the French archival materials) see H. Lauterpacht (ed.), *Oppenheim's*

International Law (London and New York, 1944), vol. II, pp. 335–349. (Henceforth Lauterpacht).

15a. Lauterpacht, vol. II, p. 741.

16. Temperley, *op. cit.*, pp. 491–493 (See footnote 3, Chapter II above.)

17. *FFAA* (see *Abbreviations*), Note No. 145/121 from Hungarian Delegation, Paris to Conference of Ambassadors, March 14, 1921.

18. *FFAA*, Allied Diplomatic Representatives, Budapest, Dérain *Procès Verbal*, February 26, 1921.

19. *Ibid.*

20. *Ibid.*

21. *Ibid.*

22. *FFAA*, Dérain in Pécs to Allied Diplomatic Representatives, Budapest, February 7, 1921.

23. Hajdu, pp. 217–218.

24. *Ibid.*

25. *Ibid.*, pp. 225–226.

26. *FFAA*, Dérain in Pécs to Allied Diplomatic Representatives, Budapest, February 7, 1921.

27. *Ibid.*, Robien in Budapest to Leygues in Paris, December 12, 1920.

28. Hajdu, pp. 219–220.

29. *Ibid.*

30. *Ibid.*

31. *EK*, p. 53; Hajdu, pp. 236–237.

32. Gunst, p. 321.

33. Mme. Mihály Károlyi, *Együtt a forradalomban* [Together in the Revolution] (Budapest, 1967), p. 299.

34. *Ibid.*, pp. 323–324.

35. *Ibid.*, pp. 301, 305 n.6.

36. Hajdu, p. 223.

37. *EK*, p. 53.

38. Hajdu, pp. 236–237.

39. *Ibid.*, p. 237.

40. *Ibid.*

41. *Ibid.*, pp. 238–239.

42. *Ibid.*, p. 269.

43. *Ibid.*, pp. 265–271.

44. *Ibid.*, p. 264.

Chapter IV

1. Arno J. Mayer, *Politics and Diplomacy of Peacemaking, 1918–1919* (New York, 1967), p. 717 (henceforth Mayer).

2. Rudolf L. Tőkés, *Béla Kun and the Hungarian Soviet Republic* (New York, 1967), p. 168 (henceforth Tőkés).

2a. Tőkés, pp. 145–146; Mme. Mihály Károlyi, *Együtt a forradalomban* [Together in the Revolution] (Budapest, 1967), pp. 466–468; Péter Gunst, *Magyar történelmi kronológia* [Hungarian Historical Chronology] (Budapest, 1968), p. 317 (henceforth Gunst).

3. Mayer, p. 575.
4. Gunst, p. 327.
5. Hajdu (see *Abbreviations*), p. 290.
6. *Ibid.,* p. 293.
7. *EK* (see *Abbreviations*), p. 55.
8. Hajdu, p. 284.
9. *Ibid.,* p. 250.
10. *Ibid.,* p. 277.
11. *EK,* p. 58; Hajdu, p. 284.
12. Hajdu, p. 287.
13. *Ibid.,* p. 288.
14. *Ibid.,* pp. 278, 288.
15. *EK,* p. 57; Hajdu, p. 285.
16. Hajdu, p. 277.
17. *Ibid.,* p. 286.
18. *EK,* p. 57; Hajdu, p. 286.
19. Tőkés, p. 161.
20. *EK,* p. 55.
21. *FFAA* (see *Abbreviations*), Robien in Budapest to Leygues in Paris, December 12, 1920.
22. *EK,* p. 62; Hajdu, pp. 298, 305.
23. Hajdu, p. 292.
24. *Ibid.,* p. 285.
25. *Ibid.,* p. 274.
26. *FFAA,* Franchet d'Esperey in Constantinople to Foch in Paris, March 26, 1919.
27. *FFAA,* French Legation in Belgrade to Foreign Ministry, Paris, March 24, 1919.
28. Hajdu, p. 267. The Bisse item was communicated by Dr. Ferenc Nagy, a resident of that village during 1918–1921.
29. *FFAA,* Dérain in Pécs to Robien in Budapest, February 7, 1921.
30. Alfred D. Low, *The Soviet Hungarian Republic and the Paris Peace Conference* (Philadelphia, 1963), p. 38; Mayer, pp. 835–840.
31. Mayer, pp. 835–840.
32. Hajdu, p. 285.
33. *EK,* pp. 54–55.

Chapter V

1. Raoul Chélard, *Le danger hongrois* (Paris, 1932), pp. 80ff.; Thomas L. Sakmyster, "Army Officers and Foreign Policy in Interwar Hungary," *Journal of Contemporary History* vol. 10.1 (January 1975), pp. 19–40.
2. Hajdu (see *Abbreviations*), pp. 341ff.
3. *FFAA* (see *Abbreviations*), Allied Diplomatic Representatives, Budapest, *Dérain Procès Verbal,* February 26, 1921; Government of Hungary Memorandum to Allied Diplomatic Representatives, Budapest, March 14, 1921.
4. *FFAA,* Dérain in Pécs to Robien in Budapest, February 7, 1920.

5. *Ibid.,* Dérain in Pécs to Allied Diplomatic Representatives, Budapest, February 26, 1921.
6. *Ibid.,* Dérain in Pécs to Allied Diplomatic Representatives, Budapest, October 31, 1920.
7. *EK* (see *Abbreviations*), p. 62; Hajdu, p. 302.
8. Hajdu, p. 312.
9. *EK,* pp. 60–61.
10. Hajdu, p. 313.
11. *Ibid.,* p. 305.
12. *Ibid.,* p. 312.
13. *Ibid.,* pp. 311–312.
14. *EK,* p. 63; Hajdu, pp. 303–309.
15. *Ibid.,* p. 62.
16. *Ibid.,* p. 47.
17. Hajdu, p. 302.
18. *Ibid.,* pp. 322, 308.
19. *Ibid.,* p. 302.
20. Péter Gunst (ed.), *Magyar történelmi kronológia* [Hungarian Historical Chronology] (Budapest, 1968), p. 340.
21. *EK,* p. 63.
22. *FFAA,* Dérain in Pécs to Allied Diplomatic Representatives, Budapest, October 31, 1920.
23. *EK,* p. 59; Hajdu, p. 302.
24. *EK,* p. 62.
25. *Ibid.,* p. 59.
26. Hajdu, p. 303; *Munkásmozgalom-Történeti Lexikon* [Lexicon of the History of the Workers' Movement] (Budapest, 1972), p. 120.
27. Hajdu, p. 315.
28. *Ibid.,* pp. 306–307.
29. *EK,* pp. 59–60.
30. *FFAA,* Dérain in Pécs to Robien in Budapest, February 7, 1921; Hajdu, p. 60 n.21.
31. Hajdu, pp. 306–307.
32. *EK,* p. 61; *FFAA,* Conference of Allied Diplomatic Representatives, Budapest, Dérain, *Procès Verbal,* February 26, 1921.

Chapter VI

1. Arno J. Mayer, *Politics and Diplomacy of Peacemaking, 1918–1919* (New York, 1967), pp. 9, 29 (Henceforth Mayer).
2. Marcel de Vos, *Histoire de la Yougoslavie* (Paris, 1965), p. 87. (Henceforth de Vos).
3. Leslie C. Tihany, *A History of Middle Europe* (New Brunswick, 1976), Chapter XIX.
4. de Vos, p. 98.
5. *FFAA* (see *Abbreviations*), Fouchet in Budapest to Briand in Paris, March 8, 1921.
6. *Ibid.,* Dérain in Pécs to Allied Diplomatic Representatives in Budapest,

November 8, 1920.

7. *Ibid.*, Hohler in Budapest to Conference of Ambassadors, February 17, 1921.

8. Ivo J. Lederer, *Yugoslavia at the Paris Peace Conference* (New Haven and London, 1963): Map of Yugoslavia (Henceforth Lederer.)

9. Lederer, p. 100 n.37.

10. *Ibid.*, p. 126.

11. *Ibid.*, p. 175.

12. *Ibid.*, p. 177.

13. Francis Deák, *Hungary at the Paris Peace Conference* (New York, 1942), pp. 183 ff. (Henceforth Deák.)

14. Deák, p. 429 and Map of Hungary.

15. *Ibid.*, pp. 524–525.

16. Fred L. Israel (ed.), *Major Peace Treaties of Modern History, 1648–1967* (New York, 1967), vol. III, p. 1873.

17. *Ibid.*, vol. III, p. 1942.

18. *EK* (see *Abbreviations*), pp. 89–90.

19. *Ibid.*, p. 72.

20. *Ibid.*

21. *FFAA*, Fouchet in Budapest to Conference of Ambassadors, February 20, 1921.

22. *Ibid.*, Clément-Simon in Belgrade to Briand in Paris, July 3 and September 13, 1921.

23. *Belgradski Dvernik*, September 8, 1921, cited in translation by Clément-Simon in Belgrade to Briand in Paris, September 13, 1921.

24. Frequent misspellings of Hungarian proper names in Dérain's reports from Pécs indicate that the typescripts were not the work of a Hungarian-speaking typist.

25. *FFAA*, *Ephémeride* or Calendar-Diary kept by Major Dérain, November 1918 – November 1920.

26. *Ibid.*, Conference of Allied Representatives, Budapest, Dérain *Procès Verbal*, February 26, 1921.

27. *FFAA*, Fouchet in Budapest transmitting Government of Hungary *Aide Mémoire* to Conference of Ambassadors, November 20, 1920.

Chapter VII

1. Peter Pastor, "The Vix Mission in Hungary, 1918–1919: A Re-examination," *Slavic Review* XXIX.3 (1970), pp. 481–498; and same author "Franco-Rumanian Intervention in Russia and the Vix Ultimatum," *The Canadian-American Review of Hungarian Studies* I.1–2 (Spring-Fall 1974), pp. 12–27.

2. *FRH* (see *Abbreviations*), vol. I, p. 369.

3. *Ibid.*, vol. I, p. 407.

4. *EK* (see *Abbreviations*), p. 191; *FFAA* (see *Abbreviations*), Conference of Allied Diplomatic Representatives, Budapest, Dérain *Procès Verbal*, February 26, 1921.

5. *Ibid.*

6. *Ibid.*

7. *EK*, p. 72.
7a. Hajdu, pp. 390, 428–439.
8. *Ibid.*, p. 67; Hajdu (see *Abbreviations*), pp. 331–333.
9. *FFAA*, Dérain in Pécs to Allied Diplomatic Representatives, Budapest, December 12, 1920.
10. *Ibid.*, Dérain in Pécs to Allied Diplomatic Representatives, Budapest, February 7, 1921; *EK*, p. 68.
11. *Magyar Életrajzi Lexikon* (Budapest, 1969), vol. II: "Linder, Béla."
12. *FFAA*, Dérain in Pécs to Allied Diplomatic Representatives, Budapest, February 7, 1921.
13. *Ibid.*, Young in Belgrade to Curzon in London, May 16, 1921.
14. *Ibid.*
15. *Ibid.*, French Ministry of Foreign Affairs for Conference of Ambassadors to Belgrade and Budapest, December 20, 1920.
16. Fred L. Israel (ed.), *Major Peace Treaties of Modern History, 1648–1967* (New York, 1967), vol. III, p. 1942.
17. *FFAA*, French Ministry of Foreign Affairs for Conference of Ambassadors for Belgrade and Budapest, December 20, 1920; *FRH* (see *Abbreviations*), vol. II, p. 130.
18. *FFAA*, as in footnote 17 preceding.
19. *Ibid.*
20. *FRH*, vol. II, p. 408.
21. *Ibid.*, vol. II, pp. 587, 667.
22. *FFAA*, Hohler from Budapest to Conference of Ambassadors, January 27, 1921.
23. *Ibid.*, Memorandum from British Embassy, Paris to Conference of Ambassadors, February 22, 1921.
24. *Ibid.*, Conference of Ambassadors, Resolution, February 24, 1921.
25. *Ibid.*, Memorandum of Conversation (extracts) for Director, Political and Commercial Affairs, French Foreign Ministry, April 12, 1921.
26. *Ibid.*
27. *FRH*, vol.II, p. 285.
28. *FFAA*, as in footnote 25 above.
29. *EK*, p. 72; Hajdu (see *Abbreviations*), p. 378; *FRH*, vol. II, pp. 379 ff. and 639 ff.
30. *FFAA*, Conference of Ambassadors to SHS Delegation, Paris, December 20, 1920; Fouchet to Briand, February 22, 1921; Hohler to Confambs, March 2, 1921; *FRH* I, 930.
31. *FFAA*, as in footnote 25 above; *FRH*, vol. II, 460.
32. *EK*, p. 72; *FFAA*, Government of Hungary *Aide Mémoire* transmitted to Conference of Ambassadors by Fouchet in Budapest, November 20, 1920.
33. *FRH*, vol. I, p. 530.
34. *FFAA*, Robien in Budapest to Leygues in Paris, December 12, 1920.
35. Great Britain, Public Records Office, C 2341/21: Young in Belgrade to Curzon in London, January 29, 1921; *FRH*, vol. I, p. 530.
36. *FFAA*, Transmittal from War Ministry *(Deuxième Bureau)* to President of the Council of Ministers, March 17, 1921, containing text of Linder's letters to Little Entente Foreign Ministers dated March 2, 1921.

37. *Ibid.*, Conference of Ambassadors to SHS Legation, Paris, April 27, 1921.

38. *Ibid.*, May 3, 1921.

39. *Ibid.*, Young in Belgrade to Curzon in London, May 16, 1921.

40. *Ibid.*

41. Great Britain, *Parliament. House of Lords.* The Parliamentary Debates. (Official Report) Fifth Series, vols. XLIV–XLV, Columns 322–331, 681–682, 238–250.

42. *Ibid.*, vol. XLV-2, Column 250.

43. *FFAA*, Note from British Embassy, Paris to Conference of Ambassadors, June 13, 1921.

44. *Ibid.*, Dérain in Pécs to Allied Diplomatic Representatives, Budapest, October 31, 1920.

45. *Ibid.*, February 7, 1921.

46. *Ibid.*

47. *Ibid.*, Conference of Allied Diplomatic Representatives, Budapest, Dérain *Procès Verbal*, February 26, 1921.

48. *Ibid.*, Robien in Budapest to Leygues in Paris, December 12, 1920.

49. *Ibid.*, same as footnote 47 above.

50. *Ibid.*

51. *Ibid.*

52. *Ibid.*, Clément-Simon in Belgrade to Ministry of Foreign Affairs, Paris, July 3, 1921.

53. *Ibid.*, Fouchet in Budapest to Briand in Paris, June 5, 1921.

54. *Ibid.*, Berthelot in Paris for Conference of Ambassadors to Belgrade, Budapest, Rome, and London, June 25, 1921.

55. *Ibid.*

56. *Ibid.*, Berthelot in Paris to Clément-Simon in Belgrade, July 5, 1921.

57. For a detailed report on the exchange of ratifications deposition ceremony see *FRH*, vol. II, pp. 655–658.

Chapter VIII

1. Alex N. Dragnich, *Serbia, Nikola Pašić and Yugoslavia* (New Brunswick, 1974), p. 150 (Henceforth Dragnich).

2. *Ibid.*, p. 152.

3. *Ibid.*, p. 155.

4. Stephen Graham, *Alexander of Yugoslavia* (New Haven, 1939), pp. 121–122.

5. *Ibid.*, p. 164.

6. Dragnich, p. 164.

7. *EK* (see *Abbreviations*), pp. 80–81.

8. Péter Gunst (ed.), *Magyar történelmi kronológia* [Hungarian Historical Chronology] (Budapest, 1968), p. 343 (Henceforth Gunst).

9. Hungary. *Nemzetgyűlés. Napló* (Budapest, 1921–1926) [National Assembly. Parliamentary Record], vol. X, pp. 328–330, 352; vol. XI, pp. 4, 7, 19–37, 44–46, 116, 368–371; vol. XII, pp. 84–88, 126–130, 335–338, 476–477, 480–481, 626.

10. *FFAA* (see *Abbreviations*), Fouchet in Budapest to Briand in Paris, March 21, 1921.

11. *EK,* p. 78.

12. Hajdu (see *Abbreviations*), p. 416; *FRH* (see *Abbreviations*), vol. II, p. 580, Bánffy in Budapest to Kolossa in Belgrade, July 5, 1921.

13. *EK,* p. 73.

14. Cited in *EK,* p. 70.

14a. Cited in *EK,* p. 74.

15. *EK,* p. 73 n.61; Hajdu, pp. 357, 423–427.

16. *EK,* pp. 78, 80.

17. *EK,* p. 70.

18. Hajdu, p. 383.

19. *Ibid.,* p. 401.

20. *Ibid.*

21. *Ibid.*

22. *Ibid.,* p. 402.

23. *Ibid.,* pp. 407, 410.

24. *FFAA,* Fouchet in Budapest to Briand in Paris, August 23, 1921.

25. Hajdu, p. 408.

26. *Ibid.,* p. 410.

27. *Ibid.,* pp. 410–411.

28. For a text of the proclamation of the Baranya Republic see Hajdu, pp. 412–413.

29. *Ibid.,* p. 415.

30. *Ibid.*

31. *Ibid.,* p. 401.

32. *Ibid.,* pp. 401, 418.

33. *EK,* p. 86; Hajdu, p. 404.

34. Hajdu, p. 416.

35. *Ibid.,* p. 417.

36. *Ibid.,* pp. 417–418.

37. *Ibid.,* p. 420.

37a. *FRH* (see *Abbreviations*), vol. II, p. 712.

38. *FFAA,* Fouchet in Budapest to Briand in Paris, August 23, 1921.

39. *Ibid.*

40. *Ibid.*

41. *FFAA,* SHS Legation in Paris to Conference of Ambassadors, August 18, 1921.

42. *Ibid.,* Fouchet in Budapest to Briand in Paris, August 23, 1921.

43. *Ibid.*

44. *Ibid.,* Conference of Ambassadors to SHS Legation, Paris, August 19, 1921.

45. *Ibid.*

46. Hajdu, pp. 404–405.

47. *EK,* p. 89 n.93.

48. *FFAA,* SHS Legation in Paris to Conference of Ambassadors, August 18, 1921.

49. *Ibid.,* Fouchet in Budapest to Briand in Paris, August 23, 1921.

50. *Ibid.*

50a. *FRH,* vol. II, pp. 755–756, Miloyevitch in Budapest to Hungarian Foreign Ministry, August 19, 1921.
51. *EK,* p. 89.
52. Hajdu, pp. 420–421.
53. *Ibid.,* p. 443.
54. *FFAA,* Fouchet in Budapest to Briand in Paris, August 23, 1921.
55. *FRH,* vol. II, pp. 795–796.

Epilogue

1. *FFAA,* War Ministry, Despatch from Lt. Col. Delteil, French Military Attaché in Belgrade, December 23, 1921.

2. At the end of World War II Pécs ceased being a polarized city. The once powerful Right physically vanished and, although the monstrance-enclosed, sculptured Host is still held high in Széchenyi Place, Soviet-style stars now decorate the facades and towers of the buildings which surround it and which half a century ago looked down upon the forces of Right and Left contending for mastery. In this half century Pécs has grown from a strife-ridden provincial county seat of 47,500 inhabitants to a Communist-ruled industrial metropolis of 156,000 souls (on January 1, 1972, according to *The Statesman's Year-Book,* New York, 1975, p. 1009). During the same period the populations of Baranya County and Pécs City combined increased from 300,000 to 429,000 (according to *The Statesman's Year-Book,* New York, 1975, p. 1009). The population of Pécs is reported as growing at the annual rate of 3% (according to János Kolta, *Pécs,* Budapest, p. 55). Since the late forties the presence of coal in the Mecsek massif is no longer the only strategically and politically active Baranya natural resource. Uranium deposits discovered in the mountainous western peripheries of Pécs (Kolta, *Pécs,* 1967, pp. 55, 69) have turned the city and its environs into a strategic asset for the Warsaw Pact.

INDEX OF PERSONS

EAST EUROPEAN MONOGRAPHS

The *East European Monographs* comprise scholarly books on the history and civilization of Eastern Europe. They are published by the *East European Quarterly* in the belief that these studies contribute substantially to the knowledge of the area and serve to stimulate scholarship and research.

1. *Political Ideas and the Enlightenment in the Romanian Principalities, 1750-1831.* By Vlad Georgescu. 1971.
2. *America, Italy and the Birth of Yugoslavia, 1917-1919.* By Dragan R. Zivojinovic. 1972.
3. *Jewish Nobles and Geniuses in Modern Hungary.* By William O. McCagg, Jr. 1972.
4. *Mixail Soloxov in Yugoslavia: Reception and Literary Impact.* By Robert F. Price. 1973.
5. *The Historical and National Thought of Nicolae Iorga.* By William O. Oldson. 1973.
6. *Guide to Polish Libraries and Archives.* By Richard C. Lewanski. 1974.
7. *Vienna Broadcasts to Slovakia, 1938-1939: A Case Study in Subversion.* By Henry Delfiner. 1974.
8. *The 1917 Revolution in Latvia.* By Andrew Ezergailis. 1974.
9. *The Ukraine in the United Nations Organization: A Study in Soviet Foreign Policy. 1944-1950.* By Konstantin Sawczuk. 1975.
10. *The Bosnian Church: A New Interpretation.* By John V. A. Fine, Jr. 1975.
11. *Intellectual and Social Developments in the Habsburg Empire from Maria Theresa to World War I.* Edited by Stanley B. Winters and Joseph Held. 1975.
12. *Ljudevit Gaj and the Illyrian Movement.* By Elinor Murray Despalatovic. 1975.
13. *Tolerance and Movements of Religious Dissent in Eastern Europe.* Edited by Bela K. Kiraly. 1975.
14. *The Parish Republic: Hlinka's Slovak People's Party, 1939-1945.* By Yeshayahu Jelinek. 1976.
15. *The Russian Annexation of Bessarabia, 1774-1828.* By George F. Jewsbury. 1976.
16. *Modern Hungarian Historiography.* By Steven Bela Vardy. 1976.

17. *Values and Community in Multi-National Yugoslavia.* By Gary K. Bertsch. 1976.

18. *The Greek Socialist Movement and the First World War: the Road to Unity.* By George B. Leon. 1976.

19. *The Radical Left in the Hungarian Revolution of 1848.* By Laszlo Deme. 1976.

20. *Hungary between Wilson and Lenin: The Hungarian Revolution of 1918–1919 and the Big Three.* By Peter Pastor. 1976.

21. *The Crises of France's East-Central European Diplomacy, 1933–1938.* By Anthony J. Komjathy. 1976.

22. *Polish Politics and National Reform, 1775–1788.* By Daniel Stone. 1976.

23. *The Habsburg Empire in World War I.* Robert A. Kann, Bela K. Kiraly, and Paula S. Fichtner, eds. 1977.

24. *The Slovenes and Yugoslavism, 1890–1914.* By Carole Rogel. 1977.

25. *German-Hungarian Relations and the Swabian Problem.* By Thomas Spira. 1977.

26. *The Metamorphosis of a Social Class in Hungary During the Reign of Young Franz Joseph.* By Peter I. Hidas. 1977.

27. *Tax Reform in Eighteenth Century Lombardy.* By Daniel M. Klang. 1977.

28. *Tradition versus Revolution: Russia and the Balkans in 1917.* By Robert H. Johnston. 1977.

29. *Winter into Spring: The Czechoslovak Press and the Reform Movement 1963–1968.* By Frank L. Kaplan. 1977.

30. *The Catholic Church and the Soviet Government, 1939–1949.* By Dennis J. Dunn. 1977.

31. *The Hungarian Labor Service System, 1939–1945.* By Randolph L. Braham. 1977.

32. *Consciousness and History: Nationalist Critics of Greek Society 1897–1914.* By Gerasimos Augustinos. 1977.

33. *Emigration in Polish Social and Political Thought, 1870–1914.* By Benjamin P. Murdzek. 1977.

34. *Serbian Poetry and Milutin Bojić.* By Mihailo Dordevic. 1977.

35. *The Baranya Dispute 1918–1921: Diplomacy in the Vortex of Ideologies.* By Leslie Charles Tihany. 1978.